T0361284

CALCIDIUS ON DEMONS
(COMMENTARIUS CH. 127-136)

PHILOSOPHIA ANTIQUA

A SERIES OF MONOGRAPHS
ON ANCIENT PHILOSOPHY

EDITED BY

W. J. VERDENIUS AND J. C. M. VAN WINDEN

VOLUME XXXIII

J. DEN BOEFT

CALCIDIUS ON DEMONS
(COMMENTARIUS CH. 127-136)

LEIDEN
E. J. BRILL
1977

CALCIDIUS ON DEMONS

(COMMENTARIUS CH. 127-136)

BY

J. DEN BOEFT

LEIDEN
E. J. BRILL
1977

ISBN 90 04 05283 6

Copyright 1977 by E. J. Brill, Leiden, Netherlands

All rights reserved. No part of this book may be reproduced or translated in any form, by print, photoprint, microfilm, microfiche or any other means without written permission from the publisher

PRINTED IN THE NETHERLANDS

To Professor J. H. Waszink

CONTENTS

Acknowledgements IX

Introductory Notes 1

Announcement of the Treatise. 9

A. Introduction of the Subject 10
   1. Exegesis of Timaeus 40d6-41a3 10
   2. Digression on the Origins of Pagan Religion. 14

B. Short Treatise on Demonology. 18
   1. The Five Regions of the Kosmos. 18
   2. There are Rational Beings in the Middle Regions . . 21
   3. Between God and Man must be 'Middle' Beings . . . 26
   4. These Middle Beings are the Angels or Demons . . . 28
   5. The Existence of Bad Demons. 32
   6. Invisibility and Numerousness of the Demons. . . . 34
   7. Definition. 38
   8. Wicked Demons. 39

C. A Wrong View on Demons 47

Conclusion 52

Index 67

ACKNOWLEDGEMENTS

I sincerely thank Dr. Van Winden for his critical remarks, which guarded me from a number of errors. I am also very grateful to Mr. Peterson, who has kindly overseen my English. Above all I wish to express my gratitude to Prof. Waszink, whose guidance and encouragement have always been and indeed still are such a salutary stimulus for my studies. That is the reason why this opusculum is dedicated to him.

INTRODUCTORY NOTES

Nullus, inquis, deus humanis rebus interuenit:
cui igitur preces allegabo? cui uotum nuncupabo?
cui uictimam caedam? quem miseris auxiliatorem,
quem fautorem bonis, quem aduersatorem malis
in omni uita ciebo?

(Apuleius, *De deo Socratis* V 130)

The belief in the existence and activity of demons played a large
role in the life of late Antiquity, both in practical everyday religion
and in the theoretical reflections of philosophy and theology. The
general background for this belief undoubtedly was the desire to
bridge the ever growing gap between God's or the gods' majesty
and transcendence and mankind. The religious and philosophical
views show a great variety reaching from simple faith to very
elaborate demonological systems. Of course many of these ideas had
a long and far from uniform history behind them. The mere mention
of all the contributions to later demonology would go far outside the
scope of this short introduction. Therefore in the following pages
attention will only be paid to some examples of Greek and Roman
theories which are directly relevant for Calcidius' short treatise on
demons.[1]

The word δαίμων is already found in Homer, where it is a vaguer
equivalent for θεός, generally in a completely neutral sense, e.g.
σὺν δαίμονι, 'with the help of a god' (Λ 792). Possibly in the *Odyssey*
there is a tendency towards a pejorative use of the term, e.g. 24,
149, where Amphimedon's ghost blames Odysseus' home-coming
on a κακὸς δαίμων. Hesiod uses the term in a different sense. The
men of the golden race after death received a special function:
'they are called pure spirits dwelling on the earth, and are kindly,
delivering from harm, and guardians of mortal men' (*Works* 122-

---

[1] The short survey given below is by no means meant to be a telegraphese
summary of the history of demonology. The only purpose is to introduce
briefly some of the ideas we shall meet in Calcidius' treatise. For full-scale
investigations on the different subjects related to the doctrine about demons
many studies are available. The best introduction at the present time is
formed by the lemmata *Engel* and *Geister* in the *Reallexikon für Antike und
Christentum* (RAC), volumes 5 and 9 respectively. Under these lemmata
different scholars have given an elaborate review of demonology and angelology in several periods and environments and on various levels.

123). They are very numerous: 'For upon the bounteous earth Zeus has thrice ten thousand spirits, watchers of mortal men, and these keep watch on judgments and deeds of wrong as they roam, clothed in mist, all over the earth' (*Works* 252-253). These two passages are quite often quoted in later dissertations on demons.

Empedocles held another view. In his *Purifications* he presents himself as a 'fugitive from the gods and a wanderer', one of the 'demi-gods, whose lot is long-lasting life', who as an atonement for some sin has to go through the wheel of birth (*fr.* B 115). It would seem that Empedocles did not distinguish souls, demons and gods, considering also his proud announcement 'I go about among you all an immortal god, mortal no more' (*fr.* B 112).

Quite another conception of demons is alluded to in Heraclitus' famous dictum 'man's character is his daimon' (*fr.* B 119), in which he obviously combats the belief in a fatal 'genius' allotted to man at the time of birth. It is worthy of mention that Calcidius refers to this adage in paragraph 168 of the *tractatus de fato: propositum id quod sortiti sumus singuli numen* (199.1). In that same chapter, in fact in the very next sentence, Calcidius then speaks about Socrates' δαιμόνιον, perhaps the most famous instance of 'demonology' in pre-Platonic thought, which was to become the subject of much speculation in later demonological theories. Calcidius in the chapter just quoted hints at the description of Socrates' δαιμόνιον in *Theages* 128d2-7, a passage of which he gives a full translation in ch. 255. In ch. 168 Calcidius according to Waszink's important note *ad loc.* is adhering to the doctrine found in many Christian writers, viz. that this δαιμόνιον was a δαίμων πάρεδρος or *daemon adsidens*. In the demonological chapters proper, however, Calcidius does not pay any attention to Socrates, which need not cause surprise, because in these chapters Calcidius' aim is to give a systematic account of the essence and functions of demons in general.

Up till Plato there is no systematized demonology. No more does he provide such a system. But some passages in his dialogues proved to be very fruitful for further speculation. Somewhat less important are the well-known etymology 'δαίμων from δαήμων' in *Cratylus* 397c4-398c5, the demons' rule and leadership in the times of Kronos described in *Leges* 713c-d, and Socrates' profession of his belief in δαίμονες in *Apology* 27c-d. Great influence on later thought was exerted by the myth of Er, which concludes the *Republic*.

The Armenian witnesses how the souls are told to choose a demon. Having made their choice, which is said to be completely free, they next go to Lachesis, about whom Er has this to report: 'she gave each into the charge of the guardian he had chosen, to escort him through life and fulfil his choice' (*Rep.* 620d8-e1). Calcidius has this idea in mind in ch. 154 and 188 of his treatise on fate, and also in ch. 132 of his demonological excursion.

No text in the *corpus Platonicum*, however, surpasses the importance for systematic demonology which is held by the myth of the *Symposium*, and especially the passage 202d-e, where Diotima is correcting Socrates' words that Eros is a 'great god' by saying: 'A great spirit, Socrates: for the whole of the spiritual is between divine and mortal'. 'Possessing what power?' I asked. 'Interpreting and transporting human things to the gods and divine things to men: entreaties and sacrifices from below, and ordinances and requitals from above: being midway between, it makes each to supplement the other, so that the whole is combined in one'. Of course Plato is not presenting a complete doctrine about demons in this passage, which serves as an introduction to the main subject, viz. the story of Eros. But Plato's successors had other ideas; they considered it to be their task to organize philosophy into an orderly whole, also in this domain. Thus the *Epinomis*, which presumably was written by Philippus of Opus, gives an elaborate sketch of a cosmic system of five spheres: fire, aether, air, water, earth. The second and third of these domains are the abode of the demons, who as middle beings are said to 'act as interpreters, and interpreters of all things, to one another and to the highest gods' (*Epin.* 985b1-3). We shall have ample occasion to discuss the relevant passages of the *Epinomis* in the course of the commentary on Calcidius' demonological treatise.

Another of Plato's pupils, Xenocrates of Chalcedon, set himself the task to present the philosophy of his master as a formalized 'Lehrgebäude' (H. Dörrie). He took special interest in giving a systematic account of gods and demons. In his monograph on Xenocrates R. Heinze devotes a long chapter to this part of his doctrine. Xenocrates took great care to emphasize the middle position of the demons. He illustrated this position by a curious geometrical parallel, employing the three types of triangles: the equilateral, the scalene and the isosceles. The first of these he compared to the nature of the gods, the second to that of man, whereas the third was likened by him to the demons: 'and the third is partly equal and partly unequal, like the nature of the demigods, which has human emotions and godlike power' (Plutarch, *De def. orac.* 416d). Another important contribution made by Xenocrates was the supposition of the existence of both good and wicked demons, an idea which was to play a great part in later demonology. He is quoted several times by Plutarch, which is easy to understand as the latter was very interested in all religion and theology, not in the last place in the doctrines about demons. Now it may be rather difficult to give an exact outline of Plutarch's views in this matter: in the first place it would be necessary to discern Plutarch's own ideas from those of the men he refers to, and in the second place one has to take the variety of his writings into consideration. But some points are clear. Plutarch is convinced of the intermediate position held by the demons who have the air as their permanent quarters. They take care of mankind: souls delivered from birth 'are, as Hesiod says, daemons that watch over man' (*De gen. Socr.* 593d). Not all demons, however, are good; at least in his later writings Plutarch assumed the existence of δαίμονες φαῦλοι (e.g. *De def. orac.* 417c). A remarkable detail is the fact that Plutarch does not seem to have considered the demons to be immortal; cf. the curious story about the death of Pan ('Great Pan is dead', *De def. orac.* 419c).[2]

With Plutarch we have entered the domain of the eclectic philosophy of the first centuries A.D., in which the Platonic element is the dominating force. Another representative of Middle-Platonism, the itinerant lecturer Maximus of Tyre, devoted two of his λόγοι to the question τί τὸ δαιμόνιον Σωκράτους; In the first of these (no. VIII in Hobein's edition) the author, having said that God rules the heaven and its order, continues with these words: εἰσὶ δ' αὐτῷ φύσεις, ἀθάνατοι δεύτεροι, οἱ καλούμενοι δεύτεροι ἐν μεθορίᾳ γῆς καὶ οὐρανοῦ τεταγμένοι· θεοῦ μὲν ἀσθενέστεροι, ἀνθρώπου δ' ἰσχυρότεροι· θεῶν μὲν ὑπηρέται, ἀνθρώπων δὲ ἐπιστάται (ch. 7). There is of course nothing of any originality in these words, although it should be noted the demons are given the predicate ἀθάνατος. The second of Maximus' λόγοι on demonology (Hobein's no. IX) goes further into the matter of the middle position which the demons take in the world order. Maximus stresses the impor-

---

[2] A full survey of Plutarch's ideas is given by G. Soury, *La démonologie de Plutarque* (Paris 1942).

tance of ἁρμονία, for which the existence and the work of the demons is necessary. The demons have to take care of mankind, a task which in itself is traditional. For Maximus, however, this task is directly related to their nature and position in the cosmic hierarchy. Their φύσις is ἀθάνατος like the gods' nature, and ἐμπαθής like that of men. Precisely this last-mentioned aspect of their structure is responsible for the attention paid by them to human affairs. Maximus' two essays, although not being philosophical or theological treatises in the strict sense of the word, are arranged quite systematically, so that they can provide a clear picture of an average systematic demonology in Middle-Platonic sense. That such systematizations existed is proved by Apuleius' *De deo Socratis*, a survey of such fame that St. Augustine pays ample tribute to it. Apuleius' is the only Middle-Platonic monograph on demons available. It repeats the same by now well-known ideas: the demons have a middle position, they have all kinds of tasks as mediators between men and gods, their abode is the air. In ch. 13 Apuleius gives a summary of all these tenets in a definition which in due course will be compared to a similar formula used by Calcidius. In ch. 15 and 16 Apuleius draws a distinction between two classes of demons, one being subject to incorporation, whereas the other class, on the contrary, more august in character, has been created as such, e.g. Amor and Somnus. Thus the traditional obscurity shown in this respect is removed by the assumption of two different classes of demons. We shall see that Calcidius admits only one of them.

It is a pity that in the most important survey of Middle-Platonic philosophy, viz. Albinus' *Epitome*, very little can be found about demonology. The *Epitome* often looks like a kind of paraphrase of Plato's *Timaeus*, following the order of subjects in that dialogue quite closely: thus at the beginning of ch. 15 evidently in reminiscence of *Tim.* 40d6 *sqq.* a few very general remarks are made about demons: some are visible, others are not, and the sublunar world is called the domain of their activities. Quite remarkable is the allotting of demons to all elements, except earth, the more so as both fire *and* aether are mentioned. Unfortunately the meaning of this detail is unclear, because in paragraph 4 of the same chapter 15 the sphere of aether, obviously identical with fire, is said to be the abode of the fixed stars and the planets, in other words, of the heavenly gods.

Plotinus takes no special interest in demonology, which does not mean that demons are absent from his works. They are subject to πάθη, but ever-living (ἀίδιοι) and their position is μεταξὺ θεῶν τε καὶ τοῦ ἡμετέρου γένους (*Enn.* III 5.6). There are no wicked demons in Plotinus' system, this in sharp contrast to the works of his pupil Porphyry, according to Eusebius (*Praep. ev.* IV 6), the greatest pagan theologian and demonologist of his time. Now it is quite obvious that Porphyry went deeply into the problems of demonology, but there is no systematic monograph by his hand available. Add to this the fact that Porphyry during his long career as a man of science and a philosopher held different views at different times, and it will become clear that it is not possible to summarize his demonology. But one point stands out very clearly, viz. his firm belief in the existence and pernicious working of the wicked demons. In itself this of course is not a new idea, but Porphyry has given fresh support to it by his doctrine about πνεῦμα. The souls which are not master of their πνεῦμα like the others are demons, but of a wicked nature: αὗται δ' αἱ ψυχαὶ δαίμονες μὲν καὶ αὐταί, κακοεργοὶ δ' ἂν εἰκότως λέγοιντο (*De abstinentia* p. 168, 4-5 Nauck). This sentence is taken from the only more or less systematic treatment of the subject present in the preserved works of Porphyry, viz. ch. 37-43 of *De abstinentia*. From other passages in his works we can plainly gather that he attached great importance to a systematization of the hierarchy of beings, in which hierarchy the demons were to form a definite category. Besides these theoretical reflections Porhyry, as in other departments of his philosophy, paid much attention to the practical aspects of demonology, viz. the help these beings could provide to mankind.

For our purpose it is not necessary to deal with the complicated demonological systems of later Neo-Platonic thinkers, as they have no direct relevance for Calcidius' argument. An exception must be made for the fifth-century Alexandrinian Hierocles. Both in his *Commentary on the Golden Verses of Pythagoras* and in Photius' excerpts from his Περὶ προνοίας a cosmic order is sketched which it will be worth while to compare with Calcidius' system, especially as Hierocles possibly is referring to the doctrine of Ammonius, Plotinus' teacher.

In the following pages I shall put forward a detailed discussion of ch. 127-136 of Calcidius' *Commentarius*. These chapters are devoted to a systematical review of the demons, their nature, position and functions in the universe. There are other passages in the *Commentarius*, in which one or more of these points are discussed. The following chapters are worthy of note: ch. 168, to which has been referred already, concerning Socrates' δαιμόνιον, ch. 188, in which within the framework of the *tractatus de fato* a metaphysical hierarchy is presented comprising, among others, *daemones inspectatores speculatoresque meritorum* (213.4), and ch. 255 about the voice of the demons.[3]

The investigation is based on Waszink's edition of the *Commentarius* in the series *Corpus Platonicum Medii Aevi* of the Warburg Institute (London-Leiden[2] 1975). I kindly ask the reader to consult both the text and the exegetical apparatus of that edition.[4]

---

[3] Cf. J. H. Waszink, *La théorie du langage des dieux et des démons dans Calcidius* in *Epektasis — Mélanges Daniélou* (Paris 1972), pp. 237-244).

[4] In order to cut down the costs of printing quite a few passages from Greek authors are quoted in translation. In a number of cases I have used an existing translation available to me, viz. the Loeb-editions of Diogenes Laertius, Hesiod, Philo, Plutarch, and Plato's *Symposium*, and further G. S. Kirk and J. E. Raven's translation of the fragments of Empedocles, E. H. Gifford's translation of Eusebius' *Praeparatio evangelica*, and H. Chadwick's translation of Origen's *Contra Celsum*. For texts in the *corpus Platonicum* I consulted the following translators: F. M. Cornford (*Republic* and *Timaeus*), A. E. Taylor (*Epinomis*), R. Hackforth (*Phaedrus*).

ANNOUNCEMENT OF THE TREATISE

[120a] Not satisfied with the description of the creatures mentioned above he protracts his careful investigation as far as the explanation of the nature of the angels, whom he calls demons. The purest part of this class of beings has its residence in aether, the second part in air, and the third in that region which is called 'humid substance', in order that the internal parts of the world are completely filled with living beings making use of reason and that no part of the world remains deserted. This treatise he necessarily differs, because it is of a rather lofty nature and above the domain of physics.

This anticipatory paragraph touches on some of the subjects treated in the chapters devoted to demonology (ch. 127-136). ANGELICAE *quos Hebraei uocant sanctos angelos* (173.22). As we shall see, the order in which the designations are presented— Calcidius first mentions the angels, then Plato's equivalent for them, the demons—is not without meaning. The comma behind 'angels' in the translation given above is no error of the press, but essential. HVMECTA ESSENTIA The same elaborate description in ch. 129, where it is explicitly presented as a literal translation from a Greek original: *humectae substantiae, quam Graeci hygran usian appellant* (172.5-6). The terms *substantia* and *essentia* can have the same meaning.[1] DESERTA This idea is favourite with the author: *ne mundi constitutio imperfecta relinqueretur* (170.13-14), *ne quis mundi locus desertus relinquatur* (172.16). VLTRA *altior aliquanto quam physica* (170.10).

---

[1] Cf. Index IIC in Waszink's edition, p. 422 and J. C .M. van Winden, *Calcidius on Matter* (Leiden 1965²), p. 221.

A. INTRODUCTION OF THE SUBJECT

1. EXEGESIS OF TIMAEUS 40d6-41a3

[127] "To give an explanation of the nature of the demons, however, is a task greater than the human mind is capable of" according to Plato, not because this exposition is unfitting for philosophers—whom else would it suit more?—, but because the examination of this subject is the task of a reflection of prime and surpassing rank, which is called *epoptica*, considerably more august than physics, and therefore does not seem to be appropriate to us, who are now treating the physical nature of things. But still he speaks briefly and cursorily about these powers which are thought to be gods, in my opinion in order to prevent that the creation of the world would be left unfinished in whatsoever respect, if he kept silent about such things. He shows with belief rather than with persuasion and proof that belief should be superior to all learning, especially as this is not an assertion of the first that comes but of great and almost divine men—after all not without cause it is said about Pythagoras: "He said it himself and therefore further inquiry should be left off". "So", he says, "neither is it necessary always to apply proofs nor a persuasive assertion to these things told by men of old gifted with a kind of divine wisdom". At the same time he exposes what Orpheus and Linus and Musaeus have prophesied about the divine powers, not because he took delight in these stories or believed them, but because the authority of the prophesiers was so great, that it was not proper to attach scant credence to their assertions.

AT VERO Περὶ δὲ τῶν ἄλλων δαιμόνων εἰπεῖν καὶ γνῶναι τὴν γένεσιν μεῖζον ἢ καθ' ἡμᾶς (40d6-7). In the translation proper Calcidius has rendered these words as follows: *At uero inuisibilium diuinarum potestatum quae daemones nuncupantur praestare rationem maius est opus quam ferre ualeat hominis ingenium* (34.13-14). There are two differences from the present passage: 1. the additions *inuisibilium* and *diuinarum potestatum quae nuncupantur*. The first of these is quite unimportant: Calcidius simply wants a clearer term than Plato's τῶν ἄλλων in contrast to the θεοὶ ὁρατοί (40d4).

The other expansion of the original text is more important. The translation of the Greek word δαίμων into Latin posed a problem; in his translation of the *Timaeus* Cicero tentatively suggested *lares* as an equivalent: *Reliquorum autem, quos Graeci δαίμονας appellant, nostri opinor lares, si modo hoc recte conversum uideri potest* (Cicero, *Tim.* p. 177ᵇ Ax). But obviously the word *lar* because of its limitations is not the correct rendering of δαίμων, which is a much wider notion. Therefore a paraphrase seemed a better solution to Apuleius when defending himself in the court of justice at Sabrata: *Platoni credam inter deos atque homines natura et loco medias quasdam diuorum potestates intersitas* (Apuleius, *Apol.* 43.2). A similar description is twice used by Calcidius in the present chapter: *de his potestatibus quae dii putantur* (170.12-13) and *de diuinis potestatibus* (170.21-171.1). In the treatise proper, which begins at ch. 129, Calcidius generally uses the word *daemon*. In this respect he acts like Apuleius, who in his systematic treatise *De deo Socratis* often makes use of the word *daemon*, although he has not given up the wish to find a Latin equivalent, as can be seen in ch. 15 of the treatise mentioned. The paraphrase is also often used by Calcidius to render the plur. θεοί, e.g. in the translation of the *Timaeus* θεοὶ ὁρατοί is rendered as *uisibiles diuinae potestates* (34.11-12). 2. The second of the two differences is the fact that in the quotation at the start of the present chapter Calcidius has added the word *natura*; this word presumably renders the Greek γένεσις, a rendering which in itself is not uncommon: in the translation (περὶ) τῆς τοῦ παντὸς γενέσεως (28c4-5) is translated as *de natura uniuersae rei* (22.9). In the present text (170.6), however, Calcidius' translation certainly is not right. Plato without doubt refers to the *generation* of the traditional gods as told by mythologists in their theogonies. About this he has nothing to say, and *a fortiori* not about their nature or φύσις; an exposition of the φύσις was only possible in the case of the visible star-gods (περὶ θεῶν ὁρατῶν φύσεως, 40d4). But the *nature* of the invisible divine powers is precisely the subject Calcidius (as so many other Platonists) is interested in. NON QVO Calcidius fails to understand καθ᾽ ἡμᾶς, an expression which Plato has used without any restrictions apart from the fact that the whole paragraph 40d6-41a3 is "purely, though politely, ironical", as Taylor justly remarks.[1] This subtle irony is lost on Calcidius, and even a

---

[1] A. E. Taylor, *A Commentary on Plato's Timaeus* (Oxford 1928), p. 245.

literal interpretation is impossible for him. How could anything be too difficult for a philosopher? So he forces himself to a complicated explanation, which in fact implies a change in his translation: on second thoughts he renders καθ' ἡμᾶς with *nobis (nunc) conveniens* (170.10-11). PRIMARIAE SVPERVECTAEQVE In my opinion to be taken with *contemplationis* rather than with *istius rei*. It is the kind of science which calls for attention here rather than the subject itself. EPOPTICA The same word is used in ch. 272, where two kinds of *disputatio* are discerned: *haec naturalis, illa epoptica disputatio est* (277.5), the latter being defined as *quae ex sincerissimae rerum scientiae fonte manat*. Lobeck, *Aglaophamus*, p. 126, refers to that chapter, adding the following remark: "philosophiae naturali contra ponit disputationem epopticam id est metaphysicam". It is perhaps worth remarking that according to the Thesaurus these are the only places where the word *epopticus* can be found in a Latin text (*TLL* V 697). Its provenance is not difficult to understand: "ἐποπτεία is the highest degree of initiation into the Eleusinian mysteries. The application of this term to the knowledge of the most sublime objects of philosophy is clear".[2] For other instances of this imagery I refer to Waszink's exegetical apprararatus *ad loc.*,[3] to which the following text may be added as an example from Stoic philosophy: Χρύσιππος δέ φησι τοὺς περὶ τῶν θείων λόγους εἰκότως καλεῖσθαι τελετάς. (*SVF* II 1008). Ultimately the metaphor goes back to Plato, *Symposium* 210a: τὰ δὲ τέλεα καὶ ἐποπτικά, the objects of the highest order, for which Diotima's introduction in τὰ ἐρωτικά only served as propaedeutics.[4] TAMEN With the

---

[2] Van Winden, *o.c.*, p. 45.

[3] The definition given by Origen in the prologue of his commentary on the Song of Songs is interesting. Origen discerns *four disciplinae: rationalis, moralis, naturalis, inspectiua*. The last-mentioned is defined as follows: *Inspectiua dicitur, qua supergressi uisibilia de diuinis aliquid et caelestibus contemplamur eaque mente sola intuemur, quoniam corporeum supergrediuntur adspectum* (*Comm. in Cant. Cant.* 75.21-23 Baehrens); *inspectiua* is Latin for *enoptice*, which term is used at the start of the paragraph. (The correct text might well be *epopticen*. This reading is defended by J. Kirchmeyer, *Origène, Commentaire sur le Cantique, prol.*, in: Studia Patristica, Vol. X, Berlin 1970, pp. 230-235.)

[4] From ch. 272, a few words of which were quoted in the text above, it may be inferred that the term *contemplatio epoptica* has the *Parmenides* of Plato in view, whereas by the *contemplatio physica* the *Timaeus* is meant; cf. Proclus *in Plat. Tim. comm.* I 13.4-6 Diehl: ὁ μὲν Παρμενίδης τὴν περὶ τῶν νοητῶν πραγματείαν περιείληφεν, ὁ δὲ Τίμαιος τὴν τῶν ἐγκοσμίων, and Proclus *in Plat. Parm. comm.* col. 617.23-618.2 Cousin, where Proclus is praying the gods παρασκευὴν ἐνθεῖναί μοι τελείαν εἰς τὴν μετουσίαν τῆς ἐποπτικωτάτης τοῦ

idea that he has now satisfactorily delimitated the meaning of καθ' ἡμᾶς Calcidius turns to a discussion of the contents of Plato's short paragraph on the gods of mythology. NE ..... IMPERFECTA Indeed the principle leading the Demiurge in his creative work was: 'that (the universe) might be in the fullest measure a living being whole and complete, of complete parts' (Tim. 32d1-2); cf. also 'And in order that the universe which had been created in the likeness of the intelligible living creature might be rendered complete ...' (Diog. Laert. III 74). CREDVLE ..... PERSVADENTER There certainly seems to be some Greek quibble with the verb πείθειν and its medium πείθεσθαι behind this opposition. Calcidius is much interested in Plato's insistence on believing in this paragraph. This is evident already in the translation, where apart from the equivalents πειστέον—credamus, ἀπιστεῖν—non credi and πιστευτέον—credendum he twice, at the beginning and at the end, suo Marte adds the word credulitas (cf. the passage 34.13-35.2). Besides it should be noted that Calcidius emphasizes the element of belief even more by saying that Plato's own insistence on this notion is due to credulity rather than to the desire to persuade and to prove. ERGO This is an explanatory paraphrase of Plato's 'Let us, then, take on their word this account of the generation of these gods'. (40e3-4); the concluding particle οὖν is rendered by

---

Πλάτωνος καὶ μυστικωτάτης θεωρίας, ἣν ἐκφαίνει μὲν ἡμῖν αὐτὸς ἐν τῷ Παρμενίδῃ. Referring to Calcidius ch. 272 R. Klibansky remarks: "There can be no doubt that the manner in which these two dialogues are here bracketed in an antithesis points to the same Neoplatonic tradition, going back to Iamblichus, of which we have frequent expression in the writings of Proclus". In a note Klibansky adds: "This juxtaposition of the Timaeus and Parmenides originated with Iamblichus; see Proclus, Comment. in Timaeum I 13 Diehl". The only time, however, that Iamblichus is named on the last mentioned page is the following sentence: ὀρθῶς ἄρα φησὶν ὁ θεῖος Ἰάμβλιχος τὴν ὅλην τοῦ Πλάτωνος θεωρίαν ἐν τοῖς δύο τούτοις περιέχεσθαι διαλόγοις, Τιμαίῳ καὶ Παρνενίδῃ (Proclus in Plat. Tim. comm. I 13.14-17 Diehl). This statement does not explicitly claim Iamblichus as the originator of the idea in question, but he obviously took special care of the classification of Plato's dialogues, e.g. fixing a σκοπός for each of them (cf. Iamblichi Chalcidensis in Platonis Dialogos commentariorum fragmenta, edited with translation and commentary by J. M. Dillon, Leiden 1973, pp. 27 and 229).

This state of affairs is not unimportant: in the same note Klibansky says: "The fact that Chalcidius adopts it affords an important clue, hitherto unnoticed, to the date of his work and the character of his sources", and "Both the term epoptica disputatio and its application to the Parmenides are typically Neoplatonic". See R. Klibansky Plato's Parmenides in the Middle Ages, in: Mediaeval and Renaissance Studies I 2, (London 1941), p. 282, and Waszink's Praefatio, p. XCVII.

ergo and instead of the imperatives in the Greek text Calcidius uses the gerundivum *adhibendae*. ORPHEVS "Theogonies were fathered on legendary authors who were fabled to be of supernatural birth, like Orpheus, Eumolpus or Musaeus." (Taylor in his commentary *ad loc.*). Musaeus is said to have been Orpheus' pupil; Linus' name is perhaps somewhat unexpected, as he is generally mentioned as a (legendary) musician and composer. But in the prologue of his *Lives* Diogenes Laertius speaks about Linus as one of the originators of Greek philosophy, the Theban counterpart to the Athenian Musaeus, Eumolpus' son. According to Diogenes Laertius, men say about Linus: 'He composed a poem describing the creation of the world, the courses of the sun and moon, and the growth of animals and plants' (Diog. Laert. *prol.* 4). This fame must have earned him his place at the head of Celsus' catalogue of 'ancient and wise men who were of service to their contemporaries and to posterity by their writings' (Origen *Contra Cels.* I 16). This catalogue, which *interalia* also contains the names of Musaeus and Orpheus, is characteristic of the Middle-Platonic awe for authorities in the hazy past. NON QVO .... CREDERET   This is rather strange. Having insisted on Plato's readiness to believe the stories in question Calcidius at the end of the chapter seems to withdraw this statement. There is no reason to doubt the correctness of the text; so these words have to be explained as they stand. Would they imply that Calcidius after all grasped Plato's irony in this paragraph of the *Timaeus*? That is unlikely in view of the 'atmosphere' of the chapter. In my opinion, the following explanation stands a better chance of being correct. Calcidius seems to expound the view that Plato did not deem these stories as such worthy of belief at face-value, but only because their truth was guaranteed by the authorities behind them. PARCIVS CREDI NON OPORTERET ἀδύνατον ἀπιστεῖν.

Chapter 127 is obviously meant to be an exegesis of *Timaeus* 40d6-41a3. As has been shown, the element which has impressed Calcidius most of all, is Plato's belief in time-honoured theogonies, whose authority should not be impaired.

2. DIGRESSION ON THE ORIGINS OF PAGAN RELIGION

[128] In that book, however, which is entitled "The Philosopher" with the greatest attention and extraordinary care he treats all problems of this kind: all things which are flowing

down from divine counsel and providence with the help of both powers and reasons in order to be used by men and to provide them with the means to lead their lives, these very things which are helping man have been held to be gods by the race of men of ancient times, because the quest of the true God had not yet taken possession of their ignorant minds. For they were shepherds and wood-cutters and other men of such professions, destitute of cultural accomplishments, who had survived the general disaster thanks to their suitable dwelling-place outside the trouble of storms and inundation. The things mentioned have afterwards been given shapes in their verses by the poets flattering men's passions because of their greed, and having given them bodies limb by limb the poets adorned them with glorious and unusual names to such an extent that even wicked lures and acts most foul were surnamed gods liable to passion. So it has come about that instead of the thanks which men owe to divine providence, the origin and rise of sacrilege was made possible; the belief of this error has increased by the fickleness of ill-advised men.

PHILOSOPHUS   Without doubt with this title Calcidius, as in ch. 254, has the *Epinomis* in view. For this designation cf. especially F. Novotny in the Praefatio of his edition, pp. 16-17.[5] But none of the contents of the present chapter can be found in the *Epinomis*, in sharp contrast to the following chapters, in which the reader is often reminded of that presumably spurious dialogue. Obviously Calcidius has misunderstood his source.

An even greater problem is the purpose of the present chapter in relation to the whole *tractatus de daemonibus*. The preceding chapter has provided some explanations of Plato's paragraph, and in ch. 129-136 in connection with that paragraph a short systematic survey of demonology is given. In fact the opening sentence of ch. 129 links up extremely well with the end of ch. 127; Calcidius' train of thought would be: "these were Plato's remarks about demons, remarks due to belief, not to philosophy; let us now turn to a philosophically and rationally acceptable discussion, a true account, a *uera ratio*". In this case *ad praesens* would mean "in the passage which we were discussing just now", and *ratio* would be very much in opposition to *credulitas*. When all this is true, chapter 128 would have to be taken as a later addition by the author or his

---

[5] F. Novotny, *Platonis Epinomis commentariis illustrata* (Prague 1960).

source, if indeed not as an interpolation by someone else. The latter
possibility is not attractive; too many texts have thus been explained away in the history of philology. The former hypothesis,
however, should not be ruled out because of the following argument.
The rather negative treatment of popular religion, culminating in
the use of words as *sacrilegium* and *error* contrasts remarkably with
the cooler, neutral, even positive tone in the chapters on demonology. Special attention should be paid to the expression *obnoxios
passioni* (171.16). In the present chapter these words are used very
disapprovingly; in ch. 131 the same expression is used three times
(173.8, 15, 17), each time in an impartial way, as a definition. But
even more notable is the very positive elucidation of the expression:
affectus nobis quoque consulit (173.20) and *patibile uero quia consulit*
(175.20). So the same description in ch. 128 is used with disgust, in
ch. 131 with praise. Because of this it seems quite reasonable to
regard ch. 128 as an addition, or rather as a kind of digression. If
indeed it is such a digression, it should be said that it has been very
aptly joined up with the preceding chapter: instead of speaking
only *breuiter et strictim* (170.12) Plato in another text treats the
problems, all of them at that, *summa diligentia praecipuaque cura*
(171.4-5). The motive for the addition might be found in the
prisci mentioned in ch. 127. In the present chapter, too, the *prisci
homines* are said to be responsible for the development of religion.
But whereas the *prisci* of ch. 127 were said to be in possession of a
superior, almost divine knowledge—a statement which seems to
surprise Calcidius—, in ch. 128 the ignorance of the *prisci* in
question is stressed and used as an excuse for their aberrations.

AD VSVM HOMINVM   cf. Cicero *De natura deorum* I 38: *At Persaeus,
eiusdem Zenonis auditor, eos esse habitos deos a quibus aliqua magna
utilitas ad uitae cultum esset inuenta, ipsasque res utiles et salutares
deorum esse uocabulis nuncupatas, ut ne hoc quidem diceret, illa
inuenta esse deorum, sed ipsa diuina.* Persaeus seems to have bor-
rowed this view from the sophist Prodicus, about whom the following is said in Cicero's *De natura deorum*: *Quid? Prodicus Cius,
qui ea quae prodessent hominum uitae deorum in numero habita esse
dixit, quam tandem religionem reliquit?* (I 118). Persaeus' dependence
on Prodicus is explicitly mentioned in one of the texts quoted in
Diels *fr.* B5 (= *SVF* I 448), to which Waszink refers in his apparatus exegeticus. Possibly Prodicus distinguished two stages in
the development of religion: 1. food and other necessities of life are
held to be gods; 2. the inventors and discoverers of these neces-

sities are divine persons.[6] Calcidius seems to be interested only in
the first of these stages: the *prisci* considered all that is useful or
necessary for man and lends him a helping hand (*haec ipsa quae
auxiliantur*), to be gods. Perhaps the second stage is not wholly
forgotten. There is no question of any human inventors; instead of
these one finds the powers and rational workings [7] of Providence.[8]
ENIM   This explains why the word *rudis* was used in the preceding
sentence. POETAE   It is of course a well-known fact that the
productions of poets in the domain of mythology and religion were
not popular with Plato. But in the present paragraph worse things
are imputed to the poets than was the case in the texts of Plato to
which Waszink refers. In those passages Plato criticizes the traditional stories about the gods because of the immoral aspects of
these myths. Quarrels, fights, thefts, robberies and the like are to
be expunged from mythology. Calcidius' reproaches are more
violent. He does not accuse the poets because they ascribe immoral
acts to the gods, but inasmuch as they are even said to personify
these acts and to raise them to the stature of gods. This accusation
is consistent with the general idea of the paragraph. Just as Calcidius does not say anything about the inventors of salutary things
being called divine beings but rather says these things themselves
are considered to be gods, in this case, too, the objection is not
against the fact that the authors of these acts are called gods, but
against the view which holds these acts themselves to be gods.
This idea certainly is not original; it can be found in Cicero *De
natura deorum* I 38: *res sordidas atque deformis deorum honore af-
ficere* and III 63: *tantus error fuit ut perniciosis etiam rebus non
nomen deorum tribueretur sed etiam sacra constituerentur*. Among
others are cited *Cupido, Voluptas* and *Venus*.[9] The same complaint
against this aspect of mythology is lodged by Theodoretus Cyr-
rhensis: "Some people even without restraint have called the
most shameful passions 'gods' .... and they have imparted their
gifts of honour to them as if they were gods" (*Graec. aff. cur.* III 5;
cf. also III 49 *sqq.*).

---

[6] For further information cf. Pease's notes on Cicero, *De nat. deorum* I 38
and I 118.

[7] In ch. 268, the opening paragraph of the *tractatus de silua*, Calcidius
mentions the *prouidae rationes* (273.14).

[8] Cf. Plutarch *De Is. et Os.* 378a, where a distinction is drawn between
πρόνοια and her δυνάμεις ὑπουργοί.

[9] Cf. Plinius *Nat. Hist.* II 14 *sqq.* and Pease's notes on Cicero *De nat.
deorum* II 61.

B. SHORT TREATISE ON DEMONOLOGY

1. THE FIVE REGIONS OF THE KOSMOS

[129] For the moment Plato has discussed this much about the race of demons, yet it is our task to give a brief exposition of the true system of demonology, although not in all particulars. This system is as follows. Plato also says there are five regions or places in the world which can contain living beings, and which have some reciprocal difference in position because of the difference of the bodies inhabiting these same places. For he says that the highest place belongs to bright fire; next to this is the sphere of aether, of which the substance equally is fire, but considerably more dense than that higher heavenly fire, next comes air, after that the humid substance called '*hygra usia*' by the Greeks, which is a denser condition of air, so that it is the air which men breathe, the lowest and farthest place belongs to earth. Further the difference in place can also be found in the respective dimensions: the heavenly sphere is largest, as it receives all things within its encircling, the smallest belongs to earth, because it is surrounded by all bodies, and the size of the others in the middle is analogous.

PLATO DICIT   In this and the next chapters one is often reminded of the *Epinomis*. In that spurious dialogue aether, Aristotle's 'fifth body',[1] is introduced into Plato's world-system as expounded in the *Timaeus*, an introduction which involves a great loss of status. In Aristotle's system αἰθήρ is not put on the same level as the four 'normal' elements. On the contrary, it is wholly different from earth, fire, air and water. This is also evident from its name, which according to Aristotle is rightly explained as a derivation from ἀεὶ θεῖν and not from αἴθεσθαι.[2] This etymology is in neat accordance with the very essence of aether, which contrary to the movements of the other elements is provided with a continuous circular motion,

---

[1] This term is not used by Aristotle himself. He rather called aither the *first* body.

[2] Ps. Aristoteles *De mundo* 392a5-9. The same idea is also put forward by Plato: ἀεὶ θεῖ περὶ τὸν ἀέρα ῥέων (*Cratyl.* 410b7). But in Plato's case this etymology has no further role to play in his physics.

indeed the motion of heaven and the stars. In Aristotle's system
the singular character of the stars calls for a special body, completely distinct from the four well-known time-honoured elements.
Aether as an element or part of an element or as another name for
one of the elements, fire or air, had already been included in their
physics by various thinkers.[3] But Aristotle, as we have seen, attributed a fundamentally new function to aether, his fifth element
or rather the *first* body, as he called it himself. In the *Epinomis*,
however, aether is treated as the equal of the other elements. This
change at once raises the question: "What is the nature of aether?".
For Aristotle this problem did not exist; in his theory aether is a
body apart from the others, which are subject to ordinary human
observation. It has its own essence and qualities, not to be compared
with the other four. But as soon as aether is given a place in the
well-known collection of elements, one is fully justified in inquiring
into its nature. The usual answer seems to have been: "aether is a
kind of fire", an answer which is in harmony with the etymology
rejected by Aristotle, viz. αἰθήρ is derived from αἴθεσθαι. What
kind of fire? The finest and purest part of fire according to Apuleius,
who in his *De deo Socratis* locates the stars *sursum in aethere id est
in ipso liquidissimo ignis ardore* (ch. 8). In this Apuleius agrees
with normal Middle-Platonic doctrine: 'aether has its place in the
outermost parts of the universe, it is divided into the sphere of the
fixed stars and into that of the planets; after these comes the sphere
of the air, and in the middle the earth with its humidity' (Albinos,
Epitome XV 4). In this way Plato and Aristotle are brought into
accordance; both are right, Plato, who put the stars in the region
of fire and Aristotle, who introduced aether as the abode of the
stars, for aether is a kind of fire, albeit the purest.   DIFFERENTIAM
The five spheres in some respects are rather sharply distinguished:
they each have their own place because of the difference of the
bodies finding their abode in them. The different locality of the
spheres in its turn is responsible for the disparity in sizes, as is
shown at the end of the chapter. So the inhabitants of the spheres
are most important; to them a sphere owes its place and as a result
of that its size. The importance of these seemingly simple reflections can be shown as follows. As long as the stars are said to abide
in the region of aether, aether has to take the highest position,

---

[3] Cf. J. H. Waszink's article *Aether* in RAC I, col. 150-158.

whether it has its own peculiar qualities (Aristotle) or is considered to be the purest part of fire (Apuleius). At the same time aether is no longer available as an abode for any other beings, such as the demons. But once fire without further addition is mentioned as the dwelling-place of the stars, fire takes the first place and aether almost inevitably the second. Now in this case one might put forward the suggestion that aether is a kind of air, a suggestion which even could be founded on a passage in the *Timaeus*: 'And so with air: there is the brightest and clearest kind called 'aether'' (58d1-2). The etymology of αἰθήρ as derived from αἴθεσθαι, however, and the fact that in Stoic philosophy, too, aether is equated with fire [4] make their influence felt. Aether has to be a kind of fire and if, as in the present text, it is not fire of a higher kind, then it has at least to be a lesser variety of fire, which procures the possibility that other creatures than the stars can dwell in aether. CRAS-SIOREM As has been stated, the five spheres each have their own place and size. But as regards their qualities they are not so clearly distinguished: indeed there seems to be a gradual transition. According to an old tradition harking back to Anaximenes such transitions were the result of πύκνωσις and μάνωσις, condensation and rarefaction. Plato, too, in a paragraph of the *Timaeus* devoted to this subject uses similar terms, and in fact also the verb πυκνοῦ-σθαι, which Calcidius in his translation has rendered with *crassior fieri*.[5] This proves that in the present passage the use of the word *crassior* refers to this πύκνωσις. Now when fire has reached a state of condensation it takes the shape of air, as Plato says: ..... συγκριθὲν καὶ κατασβεσθὲν εἰς ἰδέαν τε ἀπιὸν αὖθις ἀέρος πῦρ (47c3), *rursumque extinctus ignis aera corpulentior factus instituit* (Calc. *transl.* 47.2-3). In the present chapter such a transition is not mentioned. Air is introduced as an entity in its own right, water being its condensed form. This seems to result in a tripartition: fire (including aether)—air (coupled with water)—earth. In the rest of the treatise, however, aether certainly does not belong to the highest part of the kosmos. Otherwise the demons, whose nature is ethereal, would belong to the sphere of the star-gods and they would not be able to fulfil their function as mediators. Because of

---

[4] E.g. ὅτι ὁ αἰθήρ, ἱερὸν πῦρ, φλόξ ἐστιν ἄσβεστος, ὡς καὶ αὐτὸ δηλοῖ τοὔνομα, παρὰ τὸ αἴθειν, ὃ δὴ καίειν ἐστὶ κατὰ γλῶτταν, εἰρημένον. (*SVF* II 664); cf. also *SVF* II 527, II 580, II 642, II 1067.

[5] ἀέρα συνιόντα καὶ πυκνούμενον (49c4): *aer crassior factus* (47.3).

this state of affairs aether rather has to be taken together with air and water. The problem may be summarized as follows:

1. aether is incorporated in the collection of elements;
2. aether is a kind and a part of fire (αἴθεσθαι !);
3. it is not the highest part of fire;
4. ergo it is of an inferior, condensed sort;
5. in the ordinary series of transitions this state of fire in fact is called air.

The conclusion must be that the manner in which in this chapter aether is given a place in the traditional system of elements is not very convincing. The elaboration of the simple datum in the *Epinomis* that aether has to be taken as the second element in the order of elements has not fully succeeded. CRASSIOR .... FACTVS These curious statements are difficult to understand. Possibly the Neo-Platonic entity πνεῦμα figures at the background, viz. in such a way that we might have to interpret the words *aer quem spirant* as a sort of circumscription of the word *spiritus*, a Latin rendering of πνεῦμα. In Porphyry's view the 'pneumatic' vehicle of the soul by thickening (παχύνεσθαι, *crassior*) becomes moistened. For further comments I refer to the note on *obesi corporis* (ch. 135, 176.8, see below p. 40). RATIONEM CONTINVI COMPETENTIS The same expression is used quite often in the first part of the *Commentarius*; cf. Index II B in Waszink's edition. The expression renders ἀναλογία: *et haec est analogia, id est ratio continui competentis* (72,13).

2. THERE ARE RATIONAL BEINGS IN THE MIDDLE REGIONS

[130] Now when the outermost boundaries < of the universe>, that is to say the highest and the lowest, are filled with the presence of living beings fitting for their nature, I mean beings making use of reason—the heavenly region with the stars, the earth with men—, consequently also the rest of the places, the regions in the middle, must be held to be filled with rational beings, in order to leave no place in the world deserted. For it is indeed senseless that men, who are inhabiting the lowest region of the world, with a perishable body and a mind which, in the grip of insanity and shorn of purity, is filled with repentance because of the fickleness of their emotions, different emotions satisfying them at different times, (that men) are held to be rational beings, and on the other hand to think that stars,

endowed with a sensible nature and not liable to any repentance because of the eternal consistency of their acts, having a pure and not in the least dissoluble body, since they dwell in the outermost regions of fire, which envelops all things, (that stars) have no soul and even are devoid of life.

With this state of things is also in accordance the statement of the Hebrews, who assert that God, who organized the world, to the sun enjoined as its duty to reign the day, to the moon to guard the night, and also arranged the other stars as the limits of time and the signs of the years, as marks, too, of future events. All these would certainly not be able to keep so obediently within bounds, to move so sensibly, so perpetually and continuously without a rational, let us rather say without a most wise ruler.

In my opinion the framework of this paragraph is somewhat surprising. Its purpose is stated quite clearly: there are rational beings both in the fiery sphere of the stars and on earth, and it would be inexplicable, if the remaining parts of the universe would be shorn of such beings. Put differently: the aim of this chapter is to show that there is room for demons and that they are *animalia rationabilia*, the first part of the definition in ch. 135, the second half of this definition being elucidated in ch. 131. Such a strategy in itself is quite acceptable: first the demons are shown to be rational beings, and after that their immortality and their capacity for suffering are discussed. Now one might have expected that Calcidius in the present chapter would enlarge upon his statement that the demons are rational beings. But he deems it more urgent first to prove one of his points of departure, viz. the rationality of the stars. Having exerted himself to make this plausible in an elaborate proof he obviously thinks enough attention has been paid to the subject of this chapter. As a result of this, *consequens est etiam ceteros locos regionesque interiectas plenas esse rationabilibus animalibus* (172.14-15) in fact are the only words in the whole of the chapter which are devoted to the demons as such. It would seem to me that this is rather meagre.

SCILICET   At first sight one might think that Calcidius means that rational beings are especially fitting (*conuenientes*) to the spheres of heaven and earth. Indeed the stars, who fill the highest part of the kosmos, are normally considered to be rational beings, but earth is of course the dwelling-place of other *animalia* as well. Besides, the purpose of the paragraph is to show that the other parts of the kosmos are also inhabited by rational beings. In other words, *ratione utentibus* is not an explanation, but a limitation of *conuenientibus naturae suae*. So *scilicet* cannot simply mean 'namely', but rather something in this vein: 'of course I am now only speaking about rational beings'. The real explanation of *conuenientibus naturae suae* is given in l. 17 *sqq.*: men have a *fragile corpus* and other weaknesses, whereas the stars are possessed of a *corpus indissolubile*. NE QVIS Cf. *Epinomis* 984c5, where about soul it is said: 'soul has filled the universe throughout'. It should be added, however, that in this passage of the *Epinomis*, to which Waszink refers in his notes, the author does not speak specifically about *rational* beings. The thought that no part of the world may be left empty, linked closely with the Ancients' *horror vacui*, is implied in the idea elucidated in the *Timaeus* that the World-Soul extends throughout the whole of the world. ETENIM Probably many a reader now expects a further elaboration of the immediately preceding statement, which contains the essence of this chapter, viz. that the middle parts of the kosmos are provided with living beings of a rational nature. But instead the author takes great pains to demonstrate the truth of one of his points of departure, viz. that the stars are rational beings. In itself Calcidius' argument is paralleled by a passage in Cicero's *De natura deorum* II 42: *Cum igitur aliorum animantium ortus in terra sit, aliorum in aqua, in aere aliorum, absurdum esse Aristoteli uidetur in ea parte quae sit ad gignenda animantia aptissima animal gigni nullum putare. Sidera autem aetherium locum obtinent: qui quoniam tenuissimus est et semper agitur et uiget, necesse est quod animal in eo gignatur id et sensu acerrimo et mobilitate celerrima esse. Quare, cum in aethere astra gignantur, consentaneum est in his sensum inesse et intellegentiam, ex quo efficitur in deorum numero astra esse ducenda.* In this paragraph reasoning *per analogiam* is attributed to Aristotle. W. Jaeger, *Aristotle, Fundamentals of the History of his Development*, p. 143 *sqq.*, discusses the argument found in *De natura deorum* and ascribes it to Aristotle's *On Philosophy*.[6] QVIDEM .... VERO The author has pulled out all his stylistic stops: the enumeration in

---

[6] H. J. Rose has included Cicero *De nat. deorum* II 42 and II 44 in his collection *Aristotelis fragmenta selecta:* Περὶ φιλοσοφίας *fr.* 21; cf. also Sextus Empiricus *Adu. math.* IX 86-87.

the two cases is crosswise: men 1. dwell in the lowest sphere, 2. having a fragile body and 3. a mind unwise because of its inconsistency; the stars on the other hand are 3. wise and consistent, 2. they have an imperishable body, and 1. they live in the highest regions.

PAENITVDINIS .... INCONSTANTIAM In the *Epinomis* consistency is explicitly mentioned as a proof of (divine) intelligence; the stars do not change their purpose: 'For mankind it should have been proof that the stars and their whole procession have intelligence, that they act with unbroken uniformity, because their action carries out a plan resolved on from untold ages; they do not change their purpose confusedly, acting now thus, and again thus, and wandering from one orbit to another' (*Epin.* 982c5-d2).

HEBRAEORUM There are other places in the *Commentarius* in which the testimony of the Hebrews, i.e. a text taken from the Old Testament, is quoted as an additional proof. These texts are not part and parcel of the argument, they are rather used as an extra illustration. In my *Calcidius on Fate*, pp. 135-136 I have suggested that the author owes these illustrations to Origen's commentary on *Genesis*. In the present paragraph Calcidius is referring to *Genesis* 1.14-16, partly literally, partly in a somewhat free adaptation.

INDICIA QVOQVE This refers to the words in *Gen.* 1.14: 'and let them be for signs'. The passage Waszink quotes from Philo's *De opificio mundi* 58 shows in what sense these signs were taken. It should be observed, however, that R. Arnaldez in a note in his edition fully in accordance with the examples put forward by Philo (e.g. harvest, weather, earth-quakes) says: "Il s'agit de météorologie, non d'astrologie ou de magie". The same words from *Gen.* 1-14 procure Origen in his commentary with the opportunity to start a protracted argument about human freedom preserved by Eusebius in his *Praeparatio Euangelica* (VI 11, pp. 344-360 Mras). In this argument Origen raises four fundamental problems, of which two in fact are really treated. The second of these is concerned with astrology. Origen's principle is: οἱ ἀστέρες οὐκ εἰσι ποιητικοὶ τῶν ἐν ἀνθρώποις, σημαντικοὶ δὲ μόνον. He is rather sceptical, however: οὐ δύνανται οἱ ἀστέρες εἶναι ποιητικοί, ἀλλ' εἰ ἄρα, σημαντικοί. (Euseb. *Praep. Euang.* 357.7-8 Mras).

SINE SAPIENTISSIMO RECTORE Again the argument takes an unexpected turn. The first surprise was the discovery that Calcidius instead of a further elucidation of the main point of the chapter so clearly stated in its opening sentence (viz. 'the regions between the two *extimi limites*, both of which certainly contain rational beings, must themselves also contain such beings; to say it in other words: the aether, the air and the water must contain *animalia rationabilia*'), found it preferable to present an elaborate argumentation of one of his starting-points (viz. 'the stars are rational beings'). The addition of the *Hebraicum* underlines the importance he attaches to the last-mentioned subject. Now the last sentence of the chapter obviously is meant to put forward his view of the essence of the Hebrews' testimony he has adduced. But this view does not strengthen his argument at all: God's wise guidance of the heavenly bodies certainly does not demonstrate the rational nature of these bodies themselves.[7] Calcidius would have been wiser in using another sentence of the *Epinomis*: 'it cannot be that earth and sky, with all the stars and masses formed of them, if no soul had been connected with, or perhaps lodged in, each of them should move so accurately, to the year, month, or day, to confer all the blessings they bestow on us all' (983b7-c5).

The somewhat unexpected course which Calcidius has steered in this chapter may have come about as follows. In his source he found a traditional proof of the rationality of the stars. Being very much impressed by this idea—and perhaps wanting to give his proof of the demons' rationality as strong a footing as was possible—he carefully worded it, adding an extra argument from Scripture, possibly instead of a clarifying remark after the manner of the passage quoted from the *Epinomis* just now.[8] The explanation of this scriptural proof seems to betray the fact that Calcidius took it from a wholly different context without proper adaptation to the argument of the present chapter (viz. the stars are rational). If this idea is correct, it adds strength to the supposition that Calcidius has not taken these *Hebraica* from his primary source and that he has introduced them *suo Marte* into the *Commentarius*. Possibly he

---

[7] It might be possible that Calcidius tacitly assumes (or simply forgets to state) that God in His wisdom could not enjoin such important tasks to the sun and the moon and the other celestial bodies, if they were not rational beings. In other words: God would not deserve to be called the All-wise, if He had entrusted this work to irrational beings. But this idea is not elucidated in the text. Besides I am rather sceptical about it. In my opinion, the text certainly does not put forward God's wisdom and rationality as an argument proving the stars' rationality. It is rather the other way round: the behaviour of the stars provides an argument which proves God's rationality.

[8] Calcidius is very partial to the workings of Providence and this may have influenced his choice of the quotation from *Genesis*.

quoted these *Hebraica* from Origen's commentary or from a similar work. After the thorough treatment of the stars' rationality Calcidius now ought to have returned to the main point of the chapter, viz. the fact that aether, air and water are also full of rational beings. But having spent already too much space [9] he rushes on to the next problems. In other words, Calcidius has shortened the argument he found in his source, although he has not failed to state clearly the most important tenet of the paragraph: the demons are *animalia rationabilia*.

3. BETWEEN GOD AND MAN MUST BE 'MIDDLE' BEINGS

[131] Therefore, as the divine and immortal race of beings is dwelling in the region of heaven and the stars, and the temporal and perishable race, which is liable to passion, inhabits the earth, between these two there must be some intermediate connecting the outermost limits, just as we see in harmony and in the world itself. For as there are intermediates in the elements themselves, which are set between them and join together the body of the whole world in a continuous whole (between fire and earth there are the two intermediate elements of air and water, which being in the middle touch the outermost limits and join these together), thus, as there is an immortal animal which is impassible and at the same time rational, which is said to be heavenly, and as likewise there exists another, mortal, being liable to passions, our human race, it must needs be that there is some intermediate race, which partakes both of the heavenly and of the terrestrial nature, and that this race is immortal and liable to passion. Now such is the nature of the demons, in my opinion, living in communion with the gods because of their immortality, but also in a relationship with perishable things, because the race of demons is passive and not exempt from passions, and its sympathy takes care of us, too.

Chapter 130 has demonstrated (or rather it should have demonstrated) that there are *animalia rationabilia* in the middle spheres; chapter 131 now turns to two other qualities of these beings: they are shown to be *immortalia* (albeit in a limited way) and *patibilia*.

---

[9] One should remember that in ch. 129 brevity was promised by the author: *nos tamen oportet, etsi non usque quaque, ueram eorum breviter explicare rationem* (171.20-21).

In this case Calcidius proves his points quite satisfactorily and clearly. It is plausible to accept a middle *genus* between the two farthest; such a middle can also be found in music and indeed in the very structure of the system of elements. IN HARMONIA Cf. ὥσπερ ἐν ἁρμονίᾳ φθόγγων τὴν πρὸς τὰ ἄκρα ὁμολογίαν ἡ μέση ποιεῖ (Max. Tyr. *Philos*. IX ie Hobein). VT ENIM The illustration is taken from *Tim*. 32 bc (πυρός τε καὶ γῆς ὕδωρ ἀέρα τε ὁ θεὸς ἐν μέσῳ θείς 32b2-3). CVM The way of arguing is quite similar to that in Maximus Tyrius' second λόγος devoted to Socrates' daimonion (*Philosophoumena* IX Hobein), from which a line was quoted just now. Maximus contends that between God, who is ἀπαθής and ἀθάνατος, and man, who is θνητός and ἐμπαθής, there should be an intermediate being, which is either ἀπαθὲς θνητόν or ἀθάνατον ἐμπαθές. The first half of this alternative being impossible the second is the right one: λείπεται δὴ τὴν δαιμόνων φύσιν ἐμπαθῆ τε εἶναι καὶ ἀθάνατον, ἵνα τοῦ μὲν ἀθανάτου κοινωνῇ τῷ θεῷ, τοῦ δὲ ἐμπαθοῦς τῷ ἀνθρώπῳ (*Philos*. IX 4e Hobein). The two passages, which, as can be seen, have a great similarity, are a specimen of the systematization of ideas in the *corpus Platonicum*, in this case of a suggestion put forward in *Epinomis* 985a, where λύπη and ἡδονή are said to be foreign to the gods, but characteristic of the middle beings. Because of such πάθη these beings greet the good and honest with joy, whereas they hate evil. Such thoughts have a certain likeness to Calcidius and Maximus, but they are by no means identical with their theory. In fact the most striking parallel between Maximus and Calcidius has yet to be drawn, as will be shown in the following note. CVIVS AFFECTVS The passible nature of the demons is the condition for their care towards mankind. Maximus also holds this opinion. According to him a soul which has fled to higher spheres, having stripped itself of body (.... ἐνθένδε ἐκεῖσε, ἀποδυσαμένη τὸ σῶμα, *Philos*. IX 6e Hobein) remembering its former life now pities the souls which are still embodied (οἰκτείρουσα δὲ καὶ τὰς συγγενεῖς ψυχάς, αἳ περὶ γῆν στρέφονται ἔτι καὶ ὑπὸ φιλανθρωπίας ἐθέλουσα αὐταῖς συναγελάζεσθαι, καὶ ἐπανορθοῦν σφαλλομένας, *Philos*. IX 6f Hobein). Calcidius would not have agreed with Maximus' derivation of the demons, but in his view, too, the passivity of these beings is the basis of their care for humanity. The latter idea without doubt is a leading principle in his demonology. To him demons in the very first place are taking care of man and his world. Contrary to other doctrines about the demons Calcidius pays little attention to the darker parts of demonology, viz. the theories about bad demons with all the admonitions and speculations attached to them. Of course he has something to say about the wickedness of the evil demons, but he does not spend much space of his short *tractatus* to these demons. First and foremost he is interested in the activities of the good demons, whose actions are providential. This concentration on the providential character of the (good) demons seems to me one of the distinguishing marks of Calcidius' demonology. This providential care is closely bound up with the fact that the demons are *animalia patibilia*.

4. THESE MIDDLE BEINGS ARE THE ANGELS OR DEMONS

[132] Now to this kind belongs that ethereal class of beings which, as we have mentioned, is posted in the second place, (beings) which the Hebrews call the holy angels, saying they are standing before the countenance of God Who ought to be worshipped, (beings) with the highest prudence and an acute intellect, also with a wonderfully tenacious memory, extending obedience towards divine things, with the highest wisdom, aiding human affairs prudently, also serving as investigators and executors, called demons, I think, as they are 'daëmones' (= experts); the Greeks call men knowing all things 'daëmones'.

In the first place we have to think that these beings, superintendants of the perceptible world, are imitating (God by means of) a kind of substitution—for as God can be compared to an angel, so an angel can be compared to man—, secondly they expound what is useful for us and they report to God our prayers and they also make known God's will to men, announcing Him our need, bringing us His divine help; for this reason they are called angels because of their perpetual service of reporting. Witness to this kind service are all Greece, the whole of Latium, all countries outside the Roman Empire and the thanksgivings of the peoples by way of books preserved for everlasting memory. For the all too weak nature of humanity needs the support of a better and superior nature; for that reason God, creator and preserver of all things, wanting mankind to exist, in authority over men, in order to be reigned by them in the right way, placed the angels or demons.

SANCTOS ANGELOS   In this chapter the designation 'angels' is introduced. It is fully understandable that this word has not been brought in before: the plan of his treatise entails that Calcidius only in the present chapter begins to discuss the *function* of the middle beings. As long as the position and the nature of these middle beings were the subject of his inquiry, nothing was said about the angels. This way of thinking is in accordance with Holy Scripture, in which the angels play a big part, as can easily be demonstrated from any Biblical concordance.[10] But in the Bible the nature of the angels is never described; at most it is hinted at: the biblical writers are interested in their existence and their *functions*, but not, as Greek philosophers, in their essence. This is also evident from the name these creatures receive: they are called 'messengers', a name which explains their task, but not their being. A short passage in one of Augustine's sermons may act as a summary: *Angelus enim officii nomen est, non naturae. Nam angelus graece dicitur, qui latine nuntius appellatur. Nuntius ergo actionis nomen est: agendo, id est, aliquid nuntiando, nuntius appellatur. (Serm. de uet. test.* VII

---

[10] The fact that Calcidius introduces the word *angelus* as an appellation used by the *Hebraei* makes it certain that the Biblical creatures are meant. Paganism, too, knew about angels. In a famous paper F. Cumont has referred to Syrian theology and Mazdeism as possible sources for angelological ideas such as can be found in the theology and philosophy of the second century A.D. and onwards. These angels have functions which are comparable to those mentioned in the Bible: "les anges et en particulier les archanges entourent le trône flamboyant de Dieu, qu' ils vénèrent, prêts à exécuter ses ordres au moindre signe"; Cumont, from whose article these words are taken, *i.a.* cites two verses from an Orphic poem which have a remarkable similarity to the Biblical image hinted at by Calcidius:

σῷ δὲ θρόνῳ πυρόεντι παρεστᾶσιν πολύμοχθοι
ἄγγελοι, οἷσι μέμηλε, βροτοῖς ὡς πάντα τελεῖται.

(E. Abel, *Orphica* fr. 238/9, verses 9 and 10 = Clem. Alex. *Strom.* p. 411.7-8 Stählin).

In the RAC's lemma about pagan angelology J. Michl shows himself somewhat sceptical concerning the origin of Greek and Roman angelological ideas: "es fragt sich, ob diese Vorstellung genuin heidnisch oder vom Judentum, vielleicht auch vom Christentum beeinflusst ist". Be that as it may, the material provided by Cumont and Michl and also by Andres in his RE-article makes it clear that angels played an important role in non-Christian religion and philosophy, so that it is very fortunate that Calcidius is speaking explicitly about the Biblical angels. Cf. F. Cumont, *Les anges du paganisme*, Revue de l'Histoire des Religions 72 (1915), pp. 159-182 (the quotation was taken from p. 173 and note), J. Michl, art. *Engel I (heidnisch)*, RAC 5, col. 53-60 (col. 54 was quoted), F. Andres, art. *Angelos*, RE suppl. III, col. 101-114.

3 p. 72.52-56 Lambot). It is not difficult to understand, however, that the angels were identified with the demons of pagan doctrine, although the original meaning of these creatures is strained. STAREQVE To the texts quoted by Waszink the following should be added: 'they behold the face of my Father which is in heaven' (*Matth.* 18.10) and 'I am Gabriel, that stand in the presence of God' (*Luc.* 1.19).

The description and task of the demons in this chapter strongly reminds the reader of three Platonic texts: *Epinomis* 984e5-985a2, *Symposium* 202e3-6 (without doubt the *locus classicus* of ancient demonology), both quoted in Waszink's exegetical apparatus, and *Republic* 620d8-e1, where Lachesis is said to commit each soul to the care of the demon it has chosen and 'to escort him through life and fulfil his choice'. This text must be the ultimate origin of the words SPECVLATORES and EXECVTORES in the chapter under discussion now. It is extremely unlikely that Calcidius or his source have quoted directly from the Platonic dialogues; such passages are traditional.

TAMQVAM DAËMONES This etymology, as Waszink's note shows, is traditional. So its contents are not interesting in contrast to its purpose in the context. In the sentence under discussion the word *daemones* is used only for the second time since the beginning of ch. 129, where the subject of the investigation was mentioned. Calcidius, who is afraid that his addressee might be averse from this designation for the holy angels, hastens to add the etymology which illustrates the positive character of the demons. He silently rejects another etymology, which is put forward by Eusebius: τοὺς μέντοι δαίμονας, εἰ δὴ καὶ τούτων ἡμᾶς προσήκει τὴν ἐτυμολογίαν ἐξειπεῖν, οὐχ ᾗπερ "Ελλησι δοκεῖ παρὰ τὸ δαήμονας εἶναι καὶ ἐπιστήμονας, ἀλλ' ἢ παρὰ τὸ δειμαίνειν, ὅπερ ἐστὶ φοβεῖσθαι καὶ ἐκφοβεῖν, δαίμονάς τινας προσφυῶς ὀνομάζεσθαι. (Euseb. *Praep. Evang.* 175.18-21 Mras). I have an idea that at least a hint of this etymology was present in Calcidius' mind, for in the first sentence of ch. 133 he warns Osius not to be *frightened* by the demons' *name* (*nec nos terreat nomen*, 174.14). PRAEFECTOS At the end of the chapter this participle is taken up by *praefecit* (174.12). Albinus in his short paragraph on demons has a similar idea: God has created the universe and guards it against dissolution; τῶν δὲ ἄλλων οἱ ἐκείνου παῖδες ἡγοῦνται, κατὰ τὴν ἐκείνου ἐντολὴν καὶ μίμησιν πράττοντες ὅσα πράττουσιν (*Epit.* XV 2). This idea is derived from the passage of the *Timaeus* where the Demiurge gives his orders to the gods created by him, his 'sons'. These then take up their task, which they fulfil 'imitating their own maker' (*Tim.* 42e8). VT ENIM   Cf. Augustine *De ciu. dei* VIII 14, 1 about the demons: *quem ad modum diis, quibus inferius habitant, postponendi, ita hominibus, quibus superius, praeferendi sunt.* In this text, however, the nature of the demons is discussed rather than their function, which is the subject of the present chapter. ANGELVS   As is evident from the whole framework of this chapter and as is explicitly mentioned in the last words of the chapter (*angelos siue daemonas*) Calcidius completely identifies demons and angels; cf. also *Comm.* 246.16.   OFFICIVM   That is the purpose of this chapter in contrast to the preceding paragraphs about the demons' place and *natura* (173.17).[11] OMNE LATIVM Unlike Apuleius *De deo Socratis* XV Calcidius makes no effort to introduce Roman equivalents as *Lar, Lemures, Larua*. This corresponds with the general lack of typically Roman colours in the *Commentarius*.[12] Calcidius certainly seems not to have made use of any Roman sources. If this idea is correct, the author might rightly claim the honours of a pioneer. SIVE DAEMONAS   Up till now the author has been rather chary of the use of the word 'demon'. There is a good reason for this, I think. After the introductory remark in ch. 129, where the word had to be used to state the subject, Calcidius has successively sketched the place of the middle beings, the probability of their existence, their nature. In the present chapter he says: "Well then, the middle beings about whom I have been speaking, are the angels". He prefers this word to the word *daemones* because he expects his addressee Osius to accept his argument more easily. Only at the end of the paragraph Calcidius explicitly presents the identification, which he imagines to cause surprise to his learned friend. The first note on the next chapter will go farther into this matter. For the identification itself cf. Philo *De gigantibus* 6: 'It is Moses' custom to give the name of angels to those whom other philosophers call demons, souls that is which fly and hover in the air'.

---

[11] Cf. Origen *Contra Cels.* V 4: 'we have learned to call them angels from their activity'.

[12] The only examples are *Compitalia* (155.12), *Ianuarius* (155.14), *Iuppiter Capitolinus* (330.20) and the quotation from Terentius on p. 210.20-21. For this quotation cf. P. Courcelle, *Recherches sur Ambroise* (Paris 1973), p. 46.

5. THE EXISTENCE OF BAD DEMONS

[133] And we should not be frightened by the name, which is indifferently fixed upon the good and the wicked, because neither does the name 'angels' cause us to fear, although the angels partly are God's servants—those who are such, are called holy—partly the accomplices of the hostile power, as you know very well. So in accordance with the way of speaking practised by the Greeks there are both holy demons and unchaste and corrupt ones. There will shortly be a more suitable occasion to discuss the latter; let us now speak about that kind which according to Plato has a kind of admirable prudence and a happy memory and aptness for learning, as it knows all things and looks into men's thoughts and delights exceedingly in good men, whereas it hates wicked men, inasmuch as it is touched by sadness arising from the hatred towards the person who gives cause for annoyance—, indeed only God, as He enjoys a full and perfect divinity, is touched neither by sadness nor by joy.

TERREAT NOMEN   Cf. the note on *daëmones* (see above p. 30). This sentence is highly interesting. As I see it, Calcidius warns the reader not to be troubled by the word *daemon*. This is a common name both for good and wicked creatures, just as in the case of the angels, which appellation does not cause any fear, though the angels are also of two kinds. It looks as if Calcidius is speaking to an addressee who is liable to combine the notions of 'demon' and 'wickedness'. This is not surprising. Any Christian could be expected to make this combination. "Daemon und daemonium, die als lateinische Wörter seit Apuleius vorkommen, werden seit Tertullian unterschiedslos in der Bedeutung 'böser Geist' gebraucht. Dieser Wortgebrauch steht im Gegensatz zu der nichtchristl., philosophischen und volkstümlichen Auffassung, die gute und böse Dämonen unterscheidet".[13] Calcidius' problem is aptly illustrated by a passage in St. Augustine's *De ciuitate Dei*. St. Augustine reports that certain *daemonicolae*, among others Labeo, to whom he refers more often in demonological matters, completely equated

---

[13] P. G. van der Nat, art. *Geister (Dämonen)*, c III: *Apologeten u. lateinische Väter*, RAC 9, col. 715-761 (col. 716 is quoted); cf. also J. H. Waszink, art. *Calcidius*, Jahrbuch für Antike und Christentum 15 (1972), p. 236.

demons and angels.[14] They considered these to be only different
names for the same beings. Against this equation St. Augustine
strongly protests: *Nos autem, sicut scriptura loquitur, secundum
quam Christiani sumus, angelos quidem partim bonos, partim malos,
numquam uero bonos daemones legimus; sed ubicumque illarum lit-
terarum hoc nomen reperitur, siue daemones, siue daemonia dicantur,
non nisi maligni significantur spiritus (De ciu. Dei* X 19).[15] Such
an association, Calcidius argues, is wrong. Demons are not wicked
by definition, no more than angels are. The same addressee obviously is supposed to be very well informed about the Biblical
doctrine of fallen angels. SANCTI VOCANTVR Cf. *quos Hebraei
uocant sanctos* (173.22). Calcidius' emphasis on this epithet, which is
not used very often of the angels in Holy Scripture [16] is intended to
sharpen the contrast with the angels' wicked counterparts. AD-
VERSAE POTESTATIS SATELLITES The Bible is very sparing about
the devil and the fallen angels. In *Matth.* 25, 41 Jesus says that an
everlasting fire is prepared 'for the devil and his angels', and in
Apocal. 12, 7 Michael and his angels are fighting with the dragon:
'and the dragon fought and his angels'. In his second letter to the
Corinthians St. Paul speaks about a 'messenger of Satan' (*2 Cor.*
12, 7). As in the case of the angels, systematic theories about the
fall of some angels and their organization under one leader, who
somehow became God's main adversary, were soon developed. The
apocryphal book of *Henoch* plays an important role in this respect.[17]
ADVERSAE POTESTATIS A remarkable parallel with Porphyry can
be drawn here: in his systematic digression on demonology the
wicked demons are called οἱ τῆς ἐναντίας δυνάμεως (*De abst.* 39,

---

[14] Michl says that St. Augustine's quotation from Labeo is the oldest
Latin text in which demons and angels are mentioned synonymously (*o.c.*,
col. 55; cf. also Van der Nat, *o.c.*, col. 717).
[15] Cf. also Origen *Contra Cels.* VIII 25: 'Since then there are both good
and bad men, for this reason some are said to be men of God and some of the
devil; so also there are some angels of God and some of the devil. But the
twofold division no longer holds good in the case of the demons; *for they are
all proved to be bad*' (my italics dB).
[16] As far as I know only *Marc.* 8, 38 and *Apocal.* 14, 10.
[17] Cf. E. Mangenot in his article *Démon* in the *Dictionnaire de Théologie
Catholique*, Tome IV col. 340-341: "Tandis que les Pères apostoliques ne
font guère que signaler l'existence du diable et son rôle de tentateur à l'égard
des hommes, et demeurent ainsi dans la ligne des Évangiles, les Pères
apologistes traitent explicitement de la nature des anges déchus et de leur
chute; mais ils subissent visiblement l'influence du livre d'Hénoch et du
livre des Jubilés ainsi que des idées grecques sur les démons".

168.6 Nauck). It seems correct to consider this ἐναντία δύναμις to be a distinct and personal entity, for in ch. 41 Porphyry is complaining that people who practise witchcraft highly honour the wicked demons καὶ τὸν προεστῶτα αὐτῶν (De abst. 41, 171.16 Nauck). This makes the resemblance to Calcidius' expression even greater.   VT OPTIME NOSTI   Again a highly interesting remark: a corner of the veil shrouding Osius' identity seems to be lifted. Calcidius' addressee is said to be well versed in the domain of angelology. Well then (igitur), starting from this knowledge Osius ought to understand the Greek distinction, too. Christian doctrine distinguishes holy angels from wicked ones: exactly in this way the Greeks distinguish two classes of demons: such is the Greek way of speaking. MOX In the last part of ch. 135 Calcidius indeed pays attention to the bad demons. But his remarks are far from being exhaustive. On the contrary, his attention is hardly more than perfunctory: if one deals with demonology, one has to say something about this part of it, too. This lack of interest sharply contrasts with e.g. the chapters in Porphyry's De abstinentia concerning the influence of the bad demons. In my opinion, there are two important causes for this state of affairs: 1. Calcidius is on the whole a champion of the work of divine Providence. As we have seen, the demons' activities are an example of God's providential care (cf. e.g. per quos recte regerentur at the end of the preceding chapter. 2. Osius thinks demons are bad by definition, and Calcidius above all wants to stress the fact that there are good demons as well. There is no need for him to sketch the workings of the evil demons to Osius; these he knows already.   AIT PLATO   The last lines of the chapter, beginning with prudentia memoriaque, are a literal translation, literal that is after the manner Calcidius has rendered the Timaeus, of the passage of the Epinomis fully quoted by Waszink in his apparatus. It is easily the closest reminiscence of the Epinomis in the tractatus de daemonibus. The reason for the quotation must lie in the very positive terms in which the demons are described.

6. INVISIBILITY AND NUMEROUSNESS OF THE DEMONS

[134] Now all regions of the universe having received (demons as?) inhabitants reciprocal communications are said to be carried on by the powers inhabiting the middle residence in the world, who grant obedience to heaven, and also take care of earthly affairs; these powers are the ethereal and aerial demons, taken

away from our sight and the other senses, because their bodies neither have so much fire, that they are transparant, nor so much earth, that their substance can resist touch, and their whole structure, joined together from pure aether and clear air, has cemented together an indissoluble surface. Because of this some people think this region where we live, is rightly called ᾿Αΐδης, because it is *aides*, *i.e.* obscure.

Now, that there are many demons, is also held by Hesiod. For he says ther are thrice ten thousand of them and that they both are obeying God and protecting mortal beings. In this he does not make up their number in a fixed sum, but making use of the full number three he multiplies ten thousand.

DAEMONAS   This is inexplicable. Calcidius has never said that the demons inhabit *all* five regions; in fact this would be in flat contradiction to the partition put forward in chapters 130 and 131. So the use of the concluding *ergo* would be completely out of place. Besides, the sentence, as it stands, sounds rather strange: "while demons are lodged in all five regions, contacts between gods and men are maintained by middle beings; these beings are the demons". This seems impossible. One might suppose that Calcidius made a mistake, e.g. by leaving out a large part of his source. There are more examples of this in the *Commentarius*. But this explanation is not very plausible in view of the fact that both the line of thought within this chapter and the part it plays in the whole of the treatise are quite clear: in the first sentence Calcidius gives a very short summary of some important points treated up till now, and in the rest of the chapter he adds a few touches to his portrait of the demons. My conclusion is that the word *daemonas* has to be eliminated from the text. It can easily be explained as a gloss meant to elucidate *inquilinos*, which is a somewhat uncommon term.[18]
CAELI (l. 4) .... CAELO (l. 6)   The meaning must be different in the two cases. In line 6 *caelum* obviously is the dwelling-place of the heavenly gods, the highest of the five spheres, with a fiery nature. This sense is not possible in line 4, where *caelum* must be a synonym of *mundus*. Fortunately Calcidius himself hands in this meaning. In ch. 98 he speaks about the different senses the word *caelum* can

---

[18] Calcidius also uses this word in ch. 121, the last sentence of which reads as follows: *Et caelum quidem ita exornatum est sapientibus et aeternis animalibus inquilinis* (165.24-25).

have. One is put forward as follows: *caelum quoque usurpantes mundum omnem uocamus* (151.3). In my opinion the first lines of the chapter now put no more problems to the reader. Calcidius is saying: "As I have pointed out (*ergo*), all five spheres have their inhabitants (ch. 130) and the *potestates* in the middle part of the kosmos are the links between gods and men (ch. 132)". AETHEREI AEREIQVE Mark the juxtaposition of these two words. As was pointed out in the notes on ch. 129, in which chapter aether seemed to be incorporated with the sphere of fire, in Calcidius' system aether and air rather belong together, fully in accordance with *Epinomis* 984e4-5 quoted by Waszink. REMOTI A This goes back to the sequel of the *Epinomis* text just mentioned; cf. the apparatus in Waszink's edition. Unfortunately the Greek text is disputed, some scholars instead of ὃν reading οὐ, which has to be taken with διορώμενον. Possibly Calcidius indeed found this in his source, for he says that the demons' bodies do *not* possess enough of the fiery element to be *perspicua* (= διορώμενον?). TANTVM It may be concluded that there is some fire and some earth in the texture of the demons' bodies, albeit not enough. This is in accordance with the statement in the *Epinomis*, that 'earthy' bodies are called by that name, because earth is the dominating element in them, although the other four elements are also present: 'though all five forms of body are found in the structure of them all, their principal stuff is earth' (*Epin.* 981d4-5). The same idea is stated in the case of the fiery bodies: 'it mainly consists of fire, though it contains some small portions of earth and all the rest' (*Epin.* 981d7-e1). It seems fully justified to conclude that this rule holds good for the bodies of ethereal and airy nature: the main component in their body is aether or air, but they also possess 'small portions' of the other elements; not enough fire and earth, however, to provide visibility and tangibility. TOTAQVE EORVM COMPAGO It is not quite clear what Calcidius means. As we have seen just now, the structure of the demons' bodies is not purely composed of air or aether. Possibly the word *superficiem* in line 11 provides the explanation: in the bodies all elements are present, but the surface consists only of aether or air. EX AETHERIS SERENITATE This I take to be an example of the so-called *genitivus inuersus*, discussed in par. 89 Zusatz γ in the grammar of Leumann-Hofmann-Szantyr; an abstract substantive is combined with a genitive as a substutite for an adjective: "In solchen Verbindungen schwelgt die barocke spätere Sprache". So *aetheris serenitas* is a somewhat stronger version of *aether serenus* [19] and is meant to emphasize the purity of the aether at the surface of the demons' bodies.   LIQVORE   The only meaning fitting the context is the second one given in Georges' dictionary, viz. 'die Klarheit'.[20] The genitive *aeris* may be explained in the same way as *aetheris* just now.   INDISSOLVBILEM COAGMENTAVIT   Normally things joined together can be dissolved: *omne siquidem quod iunctum est natura dissolubile* (Calcidius, *transl.* 35.11-12). This is a quotation from Calcidius' rendering of the first part of the Demiurge's speech (*Tim.* 41b *sqq.*). The gods are joined together, but they are indissoluble because of the Demiurge's will. The present passage calls that idea to mind.   'Αἴδης .... AIDES   This etymology is of course well-known. In a passage of the *Phaedo* (80d *sqq.*) Plato several times hints at this explanation. In the *Cratylus* he ascribes it to οἱ πολλοί (403a6), rejecting it himself in 404b. In the *Gorgias* 493b5 the etymology is again briefly mentioned. In his etymological dictionary Frisk calls this interpretation not impossible, as long as one assumes the short quantity of the α to be original. So Calcidius in this respect does not state anything surprising. But whereas the usual linguistic explanations are aimed at the normal meaning of Hades as the god of the nether world or the nether world itself, Calcidius is using this designation for another part of the universe. A passage from Aetius' *Placita*, where an element of Xenocrates' demonology is reported, may be put forward as an illustration. Unfortunately the text of Stobaeus which supplies the only version of the passage in question, is corrupt and can only be repaired by conjecture: θεὸν δ' εἶναι καὶ τὸν οὐρανὸν καὶ τοὺς ἀστέρας πυρώδεις 'Ολυμπίους θεούς, καὶ ἑτέρους ὑποσελήνους δαίμονας ἀοράτους. 'Αρέσκει δὲ καὶ αὐτῷ .... καὶ ἐνδιήκειν τοῖς ὑλικοῖς στοιχείοις. Τούτων δὲ τὴν μὲν <διὰ τοῦ ἀέρος προσγείου> Αἴδην προσαγορεύει, τὴν δὲ διὰ τοῦ ὑγροῦ Ποσειδῶνα, τὴν δὲ διὰ τῆς γῆς φυτοσπόρον Δήμητρα. Ταῦτα δὲ χορηγήσας τοῖς Στωικοῖς τὰ πρότερα παρὰ τοῦ Πλάτωνος μεταπέφρακεν (Stobaeus I, p. 36 Wachsmuth = Xenocrates *fr.* 15 Heinze = Diels, *Dox. Gr.* 304b). The Stoics indeed accepted the gift from their choregos: καὶ Δία μὲν εἶναι τὸν περὶ τὴν γῆν ἀέρα, τὸν δὲ σκοτεινὸν Αἴδην, τὸν δὲ διὰ τῆς γῆς καὶ θαλάττης Ποσει-

---

[19] Cf. Apuleius *De deo Socratis* XI.

[20] Other prominent dictionaries do not supply this meaning. Unfortunately the *Thesaurus* has not yet progressed as far as this word. (Just before the manuscript of this study was sent to the press I saw that in the recently published fascicle V of the *Oxford Latin Dictionary* the third meaning given for *liquor* indeed is 'clearness, transparency'.)

δῶ (*SVF* II 1076). The difference in details is obvious, but the
general idea that the different spheres of the kosmos can be denoted
by the name of traditional gods, is present in both texts just quoted.
It seems that Calcidius has a similar idea in view and that the words
regionem hanc nostram aim at the whole or at least the ethereal and
airy parts of the sublunary world.

MVLTOS   cf. Max. Tyr. *Philos.* VIII 8: 'Great is the herd of demons: for upon the bounteous earth there are thrice ten thousand
of them, ministers of Zeus'.   HESIODO   In A. Colonna's edition, in
the exegetical apparatus *ad loc.* some texts are enumerated in which
Hesiod's words are quoted.

7. DEFINITION

[135a] So the definition of 'demon' will be as follows: a demon
is a rational, immortal, sensitive, ethereal living being taking care
of men. It is a living being, because it is a soul using a body;
rational, because it is prudent; immortal, because it does not
change one body for another, but always uses the same; sensitive,
because it reflects and no choice can be made without enduring
desire; it is called ethereal because of its abode or the quality of
its body; taking care of men by reason of the will of God, who
has given the demons as guards. This same definition will also
hold for the aerial demon, except that this demon abides in the
air and the nearer it is to the earth, the more adapted to passion.

DEFINITIO   Calcidius is fully justified in putting forward this
definition as a conclusion (*ergo*) of his argument: all the individual
parts of the enumeration have been treated and explained. The
similarity to Apuleius' statement in the paragraph of *De deo Socratis*
quoted by Waszink is striking: *Quippe, ut fine conprehendam, daemones sunt genere animalia, ingenio rationabilia, animo passiua, corpore aëria, tempore aeterna* (*De deo Socratis* c. 13). The difference
consists entirely in the characteristic Calcidian addition *diligentiam
hominibus impertiens*; cf. ch. 54 about the World-Soul: *tutelam prae-
bet inferioribus . . . . prouidentiam natiuis impertiens . . . .* (102.10-11).
IMMORTALE   The demons are not immortal in the full sense of that
term usual in Greek philosophy, but only in the limited way that
their bodies are always the same. Two important conclusions can
be drawn from this information: 1. the demons are not simply souls;
2. their nature completely differs from that of souls stripped of their

body in death; cf. especially the first part of ch. 136. PATIBILE QVIA CONSVLIT This is possibly the shortest version of the most 'Calcidian' element in his demonology, as has been shown in the note on *cuius affectus nobis quoque consulit* (173.20, see above p. 27). LOCO .... QVALITATE CORPORIS Cf. *habentes aliquam inter se differentiam positionum ob differentiam corporum quae inhabitent eosdem locos* (172.1-3).

8. WICKED DEMONS

[135b] The rest of the demons are neither so laudable nor so friendly, and they are not always invisible, but sometimes they can be observed, when they change into diverging shapes. They also clothe themselves in the shadowy forms of bloodless images, drawing with them the filth of a stout body, often also acting as the revengers of crimes and impiety according to the sanction of divine justice. They also very often hurt of their own accord; for they are touched by an earthly passion as a result of the vicinity of the earth and they have an excessive partnership with matter, which the Ancients called the wicked soul. Some men call those and similar demons in a strict sense the runaway angels; these people should not be brought before the court of justice on account of the name.

RELIQVI Calcidius now turns to the wicked demons, spending only a very short paragraph on those beings, about whom other philosophers have so much to say. Although he does not state so explicitly, these in contrast to their ethereal and aerial brothers may be supposed to possess a body consisting of a watery substance. There are three reasons for this supposition: 1. the sentence we are discussing now seems to go back to *Epinomis* 985b4-7: τὸ δὲ ὕδατος πέμπτον ὃν ἡμίθεον μὲν ἀπεικάσειεν ἄν τις ὀρθῶς ἀπεικάζων ἐξ αὐτοῦ γεγονέναι, καὶ τοῦτ᾽ εἶναι τοτὲ μὲν ὁρώμενον, ἄλλοτε δὲ ἀποκρυφθὲν ἄδηλον γιγνόμενον, θαῦμα κατ᾽ ἀμυδρὰν ὄψιν παρεχόμενον. The words τοτὲ μὲν .... ἄλλοτε δὲ have about the same meaning as *(nec) semper, sed interdum*; 2. in the series of spheres enumerated in ch. 129 after air and aether water follows; next to water we find earth, and indeed the demons now described are said to be near the earth: *uicinia terrae* (176.10-11); 3. in the introductory paragraph 130a Calcidius as a third group of demons *disertis uerbis* mentions those living in the region with a watery substance (*humecta essentia*, 165.3). Be-

sides, there is an interesting piece of information in a passage of
Aetius' *Placita*, where the author is reporting about Plato's doctrine
concerning God, who is called the father and maker, and from whom
different divine and intelligible beings originate, who are summed
up; then the text continues thus: .... πρὸς δὲ τούτοις ἐναιθέριοί τινες
δυνάμεις (λόγοι δ' εἰσὶν ἀσώματοι) καὶ ἐναέριοι καὶ ἔνυδροι. (Diels *Dox.
Gr.* 305b). Of course the nature and the cosmological place of these
three categories of demons may differ from the system sketched by
Calcidius, but at least the categories seem to be the same. The
Epinomis, however, does not tell anything more about the watery
demons nor about any bad demons for that matter. This is not
surprising. Just as in the case of the *Timaeus*, in the explanation of
which many elements unknown to Plato himself have been introduced in the course of the history of Platonic thought, the structure
and some of the ideas of the *Epinomis* are used to incorporate and
even to locate elements of later demonology. Put very simply: 1. in
demonology good and wicked are discerned; 2. the *Epinomis* first in
one breath speaks briefly about invisible ethereal and airy demons
and later mentions watery spirits, who sometimes can be perceived;
3. the two different groups of 1 and 2 are identified. More about
this problem will be said in the following notes.   DIVERSAS   In the
second book of *De abstinentia* Porphyry devotes a number of chapters to an elucidation of demonology. In ch. 39 he discusses the
δαίμονες κακοεργοί, about whom he says: οὐ γὰρ στερεὸν σῶμα περι-
βέβληνται οὐδὲ μορφὴν πάντες μίαν, ἀλλ' ἐν σχήμασι πλείοσιν ἐκτυπού-
μεναι αἱ χαρακτηρίζουσαι τὸ πνεῦμα αὐτῶν μορφαὶ τοτὲ μὲν ἐπιφαίνονται,
τοτὲ δὲ ἀφανεῖς εἰσίν· ἐνίοτε δὲ καὶ μεταβάλλουσι τὰς μορφὰς οἵ γε χείρους
(168.7-12 Nauck). The similarity of τοτὲ μὲν ..... τοτὲ δὲ .... ἐνίοτε
δέ in this text to the *Epinomis*' τοτὲ μὲν ..... ἄλλοτε δὲ and Calcidius' *nec semper, sed interdum* is remarkable.   OBESI CORPORIS
Calcidius' brevity concerning the subject under discussion is regret-
table; it precludes the possibility of drawing definite conclusions as
to the provenance of the contents of the present sentence. It is
justified, however, to adduce a few texts from Porphyry's writings,
which might shed some light on this problem. In the chapter of *De
abstinentia* preceding the one just quoted from Porphyry divides the
δαίμονες into two groups accordingly as they either rule or are ruled
by their πνεῦμα. The latter class consists of the κακοεργοί: ὅσαι δὲ
ψυχαὶ τοῦ συνεχοῦς πνεύματος οὐ κρατοῦσιν, ἀλλ' ὡς τὸ πολὺ καὶ κρατοῦνται, δι' αὐτὸ τοῦτο ἄγονταί τε καὶ φέρονται λίαν, ὅταν αἱ τοῦ πνεύ-

ματος ὀργαί τε καὶ ἐπιθυμίαι τὴν ὁρμὴν λάβωσιν (De abstin. 167.26-168.3 Nauck). This πνεῦμα plays a large role in Porphyry's thoughts and in Neo-Platonic philosophy in general. In Sent. XXIX Porphyry says about the soul: ἐν τῇ ἐξόδῳ ἔτι κατὰ τὴν δίυγρον ἀναθυμίασιν τὸ πνεῦμα ἔχουσα τεθολωμένον, σκιὰν ἐφέλκεται καὶ βαρεῖται, χωρεῖν σπεύδοντος τοῦ τοιούτου πνεύματος εἰς μυχὸν τῆς γῆς φύσει, ἂν μὴ ἄλλη τις αὐτὸ αἰτία ἀνθέλκῃ. ὥσπερ οὖν τὸ γεῶδες ὄστρεον περικειμένη ἀνάγκη ἐπὶ γῆς ἐνίσχεσθαι, οὕτω καὶ ὑγρὸν πνεῦμα ἐφελκομένη εἴδωλον περικεῖσθαι ἀνάγκη (Porph. Sent. 19.14-20.1 Lamberz). In the chapter from which these words are quoted Porphyry is explaining the position of the soul in the nether world. This position is due to the humid character of the πνεῦμα. In a better state the soul is coupled with a body which is nearer the immaterial world: καθαρώτερον διακειμένη σύμφυτον τὸ ἐγγὺς τοῦ ἀύλου σῶμα, ὅπερ ἐστὶ τὸ αἰθέριον (ib. 19.6-7). As can be seen, the humidity of the πνεῦμα enveloping the soul causes the lower state of the latter. About this humid πνεῦμα there is a very interesting statement in De antro nympharum: τάς γε φιλοσωμάτους (ψυχὰς) ὑγρὸν τὸ πνεῦμα ἐφελκομένας παχύνειν τοῦτο ὡς νέφος· ὑγρὸν γὰρ ἐν ἀέρι παχυνθὲν νέφος συνίσταται· παχυνθέντος δ' ἐν αὐταῖς τοῦ πνεύματος ὑγροῦ πλεονασμῷ ὁρατὰς γίνεσθαι (De antro nymph. 64.15-18 Nauck). In this text is explicitly stated that humid πνεῦμα is a thicken(ed) body and because of its humidity makes the souls visible. The text continues as follows: καὶ ἐκ τῶν τοιούτων αἱ συναντῶσαί τισι κατὰ φαντασίαν χρώζουσαι τὸ πνεῦμα εἰδώλων ἐμφάσεις (ib. 64.19-20). I think one has to be cautious in drawing conclusions from these texts. In the texts just quoted from the Sententiae and De antro nympharum Porphyry is not speaking about the demons, but about the soul in general. It is of course quite possible that he also applied these general reflections to demonology, but the fact remains that in the only text where demonology is explicitly and systematically treated by Porphyry he has not done so. But let us first return to Calcidius. It is worth while to quote his literal text: Exsanguium quoque simulacrorum umbraticas formas induuntur obesi corporis illuuiem trahentes (176.7-9). The similarity to some of the elements found in Porphyry's texts is very striking: simulacrum - εἴδωλον, umbraticas - σκιά, obesus - παχύνειν, trahere - ἐφέλκεσθαι. There cannot be much doubt that obesum corpus is Calcidius' description of πνεῦμα in a humid state. It is not clear why he has not used spiritus as an equivalent for πνεῦμα, but perhaps he deemed that the very special meaning in the present context would be unintelligible for Osius.

Possibly in the strange sentence added to the description of *humecta substantia* as densified air, viz. *ut sit aer iste quem homines spirant* (172.6-7), the verb *spirare* is a reminiscence of the word πνεῦμα. In that case the conclusion would have to be that Calcidius does not quite know what to do with the term πνεῦμα in its Neo-Platonic sense.[21] In any case I think it is justified to conclude that the sentence just quoted from Calcidius contains some unmistakable Porphyrian elements. So if Calcidius is using Porphyry as his source in the short treatise on demons, the conclusion could be that Porphyry has indeed linked his general reflections on the soul's πνεῦμα with demonology. This would involve an important adaptation of these reflections, for the systematic demonology put forward by Calcidius is quite rigid; the demons remain in their own sphere, eternally keeping their body (*non mutat corpus aliud ex alio*, ch. 135, 175.19-20); this is explicitly stated about the ethereal and aerial demons (*eadem erit definitio aerei quoque daemonis*, 176.3-4) and implicitly (cf. also the beginning of ch. 136) about the wicked demons. Such a rigidity strictly speaking does not agree with Porphyry's views.

VLTORES   It is not surprising that this task is entrusted to the demons. Just as the highest god does not see to mankind personally, but uses the demons as intermediaries,[22] thus, when punishment has to be inflicted upon wrongdoers, these same agents are the actual executioners; in a passage, which according to Heinze [23] provides

---

[21] For Porphyry's doctrine about πνεῦμα cf. his *Sententiae* ch. 29 and R. Beutler, art. *Porphyrios*, RE XXII[1], col. 308-310.

[22] Cf. E. R. Dodds, *Pagan and Christian in an Age of Anxiety* (Cambridge 1965), p. 37: "God has no contact with man; only through the daemonic is there intercourse and conversation between men and gods". In his demonological monograph Apuleius explicitly deals with this question; cf. J. Beaujeu's comments on Apuleius' *De deo Socratis* par. 127-132 (*Apulée, Opuscules philosophiques et fragments*, ed. J. Beaujeu, Paris 1973, pp. 212-215), B. M. Portogalli, *Sulle fonti della concezione teologica e demonologica di Apuleio*, Studi Classici e Orientali XII (1963), p. 233, and especially F. Regen, *Apuleius philosophus Platonicus* (Berlin 1971), p. 84: "Im Grunde jedes dämonologische System entspringt nicht zuletzt dem Bestreben, die Vorstellung einer ausserordentlichen Majestät Gottes gleichwohl mit der seiner Fürsorge für die Welt in Einklang zu bringen: Da sich der höchste Gott eben wegen seiner 'Höhe' um 'Niedriges' nicht bekümmert, müssen Vermittler diese Aufgabe übernehmen: Die Dämonen werden zu Verwaltern der Vorsehung".

[23] R. Heinze, *Xenokrates, Darstellung der Lehre und Sammlung der Fragmente* (Leipzig 1892), p. 81 (concerning *De def. orac.* ch. 13-15): "Am Eingang von C. 13 wird Xenocrates citiert; auf ihn geht aller Wahrscheinlichkeit nach das ganze genannte Stück zurück".

information on Xenocratean doctrine, Plutarch says: (νομίζωμεν) ἄλλους δὲ (δαίμονας) τῶν ὑπερηφάνων καὶ μεγάλων τιμωροὺς ἀδικιῶν περιπολεῖν (Plut. De def. orac. 417b). Calcidius' expression iuxta iustitiae diuinae sanctionem calls to mind the theories of the fifth-century Alexandrian Platonist Hierocles. According to Photius' summary he ascribes a tripartition of beings to Plato. First he mentions οὐράνια καὶ θεούς, next αἰθέρια καὶ δαίμονας ἀγαθούς, ἑρμη-νέας τε καὶ ἀγγέλους τῶν συμφερόντων ἀνθρώποις γινομένους, and as a third category λογικὰ καὶ περίγεια καὶ ἀνθρωπίνους ψυχὰς ἢ ἀθανάτους ἀνθρώπους (Hierocles apud Photius cod. 251, 461b13-17 p. 192 Henry). This tripartition, although not exactly the same as in Cal-cidius' or others' demonological systems, has a certain similarity to these theories. Now Hierocles was a champion of human freedom. Man is responsible for his action, and fate receives the character of retributive justice.[24] This justice is exercised by the middle beings: Ἀναγκαῖον δὴ τὸ λειπόμενον· τὰς μὲν προαιρέσεις ἐφ' ἡμῖν εἶναι, τὰς δ' ἐπὶ ταῖς προαιρέσεσι δικαίας ἀμοιβὰς ἐπὶ τοῖς αἰθερίοις κεῖσθαι, ὡς ὑπὸ Θεοῦ τεταγμένοις δικασταῖς καὶ πεφυκόσιν ἡμῶν ἐπιμελεῖσθαι (Hiero-cles apud Photius cod. 251, 462b19-22, p. 195 Henry). In a compar-able way in ch. 188 Calcidius mentions the daemones inspectatores speculatoresque meritorum (213.4). Both in Plutarch and in Hierocles the punishment is inflicted by demons (or the demons) without any negative qualification. Such is not the case in the present chapter, where the bad demons are explicitly mentioned as the avengers. The most striking illustration of the idea being discussed now is provided by the Stoa, at least if Plutarch's information is correct: οἱ περὶ Χρύσιππον οἴονται φιλόσοφοι φαῦλα δαιμόνια περινοστεῖν, οἷς οἱ θεοὶ δημίοις χρῶνται <καὶ> κολασταῖς ἐπὶ τοὺς ἀνοσίους καὶ ἀδίκους ἀν-θρώπους (Plut. Quaest. Rom. 51, 276f; δήμιος as a substantive means 'public executioner'). VLTRO Mark the pun ultores - ultro. The bad acts which these demons perform on their own initiative are the subject of the greater part of Porphyry's demonological section in De abstinentia II 37-43. Calcidius confines himself to a few sober remarks pointing out at once the fundamental reason of their wickedness: their contact with the bad World-Soul of matter. SILVA Matter is discussed in ch. 268-354 of the Commentarius; ch. 295-299 [25] reproduce Numenius' doctrine on the subject. Numenius is

[24] Cf. J. den Boeft, Calcidius on Fate (Leiden 1970), p. 105.
[25] In Leemans' edition of Numenius these chapters are test. 30, in the edition of E. des Places fr. 52.

combating the Stoic views that matter is neither good nor evil. He refers to the relevant idea of Pythagoras, with whom Plato agrees, that matter is the cause of evil, God being the cause of the good. The world is a mixture of the goodness of form and the badness of matter. In ch. 297 Numenius is said to have praised Plato's doctrine of two World-Souls, the good and the bad one; the latter is equated with matter: *Platonemque idem Numenius laudat, quod duas mundi animas autumat, unam beneficentissimam, malignam alteram, scilicet siluam* (299.14-16). For a full discussion of these *Numeniana* I refer to the expositions of Waszink and van Winden. Suffice it for our purpose to conclude that the equation 'matter = bad World-Soul' is a theory of which at the moment only one *auctor* is known, viz. Numenius, who in accordance with his normal custom ascribes this theory to older authorities, such as Plato and Pythagoras. So we may cautiously conclude that the short remark here: *silua, quam malignam animam ueteres uocabant* is a *Numenianum*, albeit anonymous. The isolated character of this *Numenianum*, however, does not allow any far-reaching conclusions. In fact it rather leaves us with uncertainties concerning its implications. In itself it is not surprising that the wickedness of the evil spirits is ascribed to matter. Are we to suppose that the relative clause *quam malignam animam ueteres uocabant* is only a learned addition of Calcidius himself or did he find it in his source? And if the last-mentioned supposition is correct, is the laconic brevity of the clause due to the source or to Calcidius' summarizing? Again, if the latter possibility is more probable, does that imply a large Numenian tinge of the whole of the demonology or at least of the part about the evil demons? Although I think none of these questions can be answered with any certainty, I propose the following view. As stated before, it is quite understandable that the evil spirits are said to side with matter. But perhaps Calcidius (or his source) only wants to prevent any misunderstanding, so that he hastens to add that matter is *bad*. In fact the only term explicitly mentioning wickedness is the word *malignam*. Although the notion is implied in other words and expressions, an explicit mention does not seem redundant. So I take it that the relative clause is added to remind the reader of the badness of matter. There is no need to suppose that this dogma was treated at any length in Calcidius' source. In any case the information is too limited to infer a large Numenian influence upon Calcidius' exposition of demonology, the more so as nothing is known about any demonological tenet proposed by Numenius. Demonological ideas are absent from the collections of fragments edited by Leemans and des Places. This must mean that he did not contribute anything of special interest to the history of demonology.[26] My conclusion would be that Calcidius, or perhaps rather his source, *suo Marte* added the Numenian expression about the *anima maligna*. VETERES Waszink *ad loc.* notes: *in primis Numenius*. I should rather be inclined to think of Pythagoras and Plato (of course looked at through Numenian spectacles), for in my opinion the word *ueteres* points to the venerable past, which was considered to be authoritative in later Platonism and especially by Numenius. Mark the difference in tenses: *uocabant* (12) .... *uocant* (13). The former is used about the thinkers of old, whereas *uocant* concerns the philosophers of modern times. PROPRIE This refers to the start of ch. 133, where Osius' possible misconception was taken away. Not all the demons are bad; only the demons discussed just now deserve that qualification; they may be identified with the fallen angels. DESERTORES ANGELOS Among Biblical testimonies cf. especially *2 Petr.* 2, 4: 'God spared not the angels that sinned' and *Jud.* 6: God punished 'the angels which kept not their first estate, but left their own habitation'. The latter text is often brought into connection with *Gen.* 6.4, where it is told that 'the sons of God (in this explanation = the angels) come in unto the daughters of men'. NVLLA QVAESTIO The meaning of this sentence is not fully

---

[26] Concerning the war between Athens and Atlantis Proclus in his commentary on the *Timaeus* reports that some thinkers, among whom Origenes, regarded this war as a reference to the conflict between two classes of demons. Numenius, however, held another opinion; he took it to be a ψυχῶν διάστασις (Proclus *in Plat. Tim. comm.* I 76.21-77.23 Diehl= Numenius *fr.* 37 des Places). Others according to Proclus mixed both explanations, saying that an attack by wicked demons on souls descending into birth is meant by the story of the war. One of these thinkers, to Proclus' sarcastic surprise, is Porphyry, ὃν καὶ θαυμάσειεν ἄν τις εἰ ἕτερα λέγοι τῆς Νουμηνίου παραδόσεως. This famous sentence indeed stresses the influence exerted by Numenius on Porphyry's philosophy, an influence which has been expounded in detail by Waszink in his paper *Porphyrios und Numenios* (Entretiens sur l'Antiquité classique, t. XII, Geneva 1965, pp. 35-83). On the other hand, one should not overlook the exaggerated character of Proclus' sarcasm, which brings to mind the fact that Plotinus, too, was accused of plagiarizing Numenius (Porphyry, *Vita Plotini* ch. 17). In any case Proclus' remark concerns Pophyry's philosophy in general; its purpose is not to portray him as Numenius' slavish imitator *in demonologicis* only. In other words, Proclus' phrase cannot be adduced as a proof that it was particularly his demonology which Porphyry owed to Numenius.

clear. I take it that the expression *quaestionem referre alicui*, for which I have not been able to find a parallel, has the same meaning as e.g. *quaestionem ferre in aliquem* (Cicero, *De orat.* I 53, 227), viz. 'to institute a trial against a person'; the preposition *de* is used with *quaestio* to indicate the crime. Obviously *de nomine* again refers to the problem of the name hinted at in the beginning of ch. 133. Accordingly, stripped of the judicial metaphor the meaning is: "there is no need to criticize them on account of the name". But who are meant by *quibus*? There are two possibilities: 1. the antecedent of *quibus* is *angelos*; in that case the sense would be: the angels should not be incriminated because of their name (*angelos*), (but rather because of their deeds — *desertores*?); 2. the antecedent of *quibus* is the unmentioned subject of *uocant*; in other words: *quibus* has to be explained as (*ei*) *quibus*. This would result in the following meaning: people who use these designations should not be attacked on that account. This last-mentioned solution seems more probable.

C. A WRONG VIEW ON DEMONS

[136] Many philosophers belonging to the Platonic school nevertheless think the demons are souls freed from their bodily task, those of the praiseworthy men the ethereal demons, those of the wicked souls the pernicious demons, and that these same souls only in the thousandth year take an earthly body again, and Empedocles in the same manner thinks that these souls become demons of great age; Pythagoras also in his Golden verses says: "When, having laid aside your body, you will proceed as a free person to aether, you will evade the state of man, having become a god of the bountiful aether". With these words Plato does not seem to agree in the least part, when in the *Politeia* he has the soul of a tyrant being tortured by revengers after death, from which it is clear that soul and demon are different beings, as it must necessarily be so, that that which is tortured and that which is torturing are entirely different beings, and because the Demiurge established the demons before he created our souls and because he wanted the latter to be in need of the demons' help and the former to procure protection. Yet he thinks that some souls which have led their lives excellently throughout three incarnations by the merit of their virtue are elevated to the aerial or even to the ethereal regions, exempt from the fate of embodiment.

EX PLATONIS MAGISTERIO   Cf. the expression *ex Pythagorae magisterio*, used by Calcidius concerning Timaeus (60.1 and 99.26) and Numenius (297.8): it may be concluded that in the present passage the expression means 'belonging to Plato's school'; the same explanation is to be found in the *Thesaurus*: *fere i.q. schola* (*TLL* VIII 90): the same passages from Calcidius are quoted. CORPOREO MVNERE LIBERATAS   This idea is held by more than one Platonist. Among others the following texts can be adduced: 'souls delivered from birth and henceforth at rest from the body—set quite free, as it were, to range at will—are, as Hesiod says, daemons that watch over man' (Plut. *De genio Socr.* 593d), Plutarch, *De def. orac.* 431e and *De fac.* 944c, Maximus Tyrius *Philos.* IX 6e Hobein, Apuleius *De deo Socr.* XV 152, cf. also Diog. Laert. VIII 32 (= Alexander Polyhistor about Pythagoras). EASDEMQVE   I fail to understand

Waszink's complaint in the exegetical apparatus *ad loc.* Calcidius says that some souls stripped of their earthly body become either good demons with an ethereal, or, it seems justified to add, an aerial body, or bad demons (with a watery body?, cf. above p. 39). Then after a thousand years these same souls give up their demonical activities and return to earth. In my opinion, the word *easdem* leaves no room for misunderstanding. EMPEDOCLES Calcidius obviously has a predilection for this philosopher. He is quoted eight times in the *Commentarius* and only in the present chapter without mentioning the full translated text of one or more verses. It is a little unfortunate that precisely in the text we are discussing now Calcidius has confined himself to a short reference only. For there is a problem. In the sentence *longaeuos daemonas fieri has animas* the presence of the demonstrative pronoun *has* forces the reader to the conclusion that *has animas* is subject and *longaeuos daemonas* predicate. In the text of Empedocles which Calcidius in all probability has in view the metempsychosis is in the other direction: the demons of long-lasting life are punished for their sins and wander into the forms of all sorts of mortal things, not finding rest anywhere, but all the time being chased away into the spheres of other elements. The fragment ends with Empedocles' famous saying: 'Of these I too am now one, a fugitive from the gods and a wanderer, who put my trust in raving strife' (*fr.* B 115, 7-8). The problem sketched is not very awkward, however, for in any case Empedocles is speaking about a metempsychosis between demons and other beings, which according to Calcidius has to be rejected. AVREIS VERSIBVS For a full-scale exegesis of the two verses quoted cf. P. C. van der Horst's edition with commentary (*Les vers d'or Pythagoriciens*, Leiden 1932). LIBER Calcidius reads ἐλεύθερος instead of ἐλεύθε-ρον.[1] He is obviously rather eager to stress *corpore deposito* even more. DEVS Van der Horst draws attention to the fact that θεὸς ἄμβροτος οὐκέτι θνητός is a quotation from Empedocles *fr.* B 112, 4. AETHERIS ALMI This probably renders ἄμβροτος. Apart from any metrical problems this translation must be due to *aethera* in the first line of the quotation. Thus the notion of *aether* receives more emphasis, and this is precisely what Calcidius wants, the wrongness of the idea implicitly present in these verses (according to his view)

---

[1] In Van der Horst's edition the critical apparatus does not mention this variant.

now becoming quite clear: man after death moves to the sphere of aether, which is the abode of the *aetherei daemones*. CONSENTIRE MINIME Two arguments are put forward to combat the view just sketched, the first one of a mainly logical character, and the second, much more important and interesting, of a cosmological nature. POLITIA An appeal to the authoritative and almost sacred text of Plato is of course normal. The choice of the passage, however, is somewhat surprising. One might have expected the choice of a passage a little further in the *Republic*, viz. 620d *sqq.*, where the souls are choosing their demons, who are to be their guards. The logical argument drawn from the text could have been the same, e.g. *quod eligitur et quod eligit diuersa esse*. But probably the treatment given to Adriaeus by the 'fierce and fiery-looking men' (615e4) is thought to be more convincing. VLTORIBVS The fierce and fiery-looking men are thus interpreted as *daemones nocentes*, if indeed the argument is consistent: in ch. 135 the *ultores* obviously are evil spirits.[2]

ANTE .... QVAM This argument based on the hierarchy in the kosmos is highly interesting. It obviously is the real reason why the equation of demons with human souls after death is strongly rejected. As we have seen (above p. 47), this equation is to be found in a few authors who, broadly speaking, belong to Middle-Platonism. It is remarkable that even Apuleius, who is the only representative of that school of thought to have given a systematic treatment of demonology in the first part of his *De deo Socratis*, holds this opinion about part of the demons: *est et secundo significatu species daemonum animus humanus emeritis stipendiis uitae corpore suo abiurans* (Apul. *De deo Socr.* XV). According to Heinze,[3] this is one of the tenets of Xenocrates, who may be considered to have originated the systematization of demonology. Heinze's arguments for this special point are not very strong. In none of the fragments it is mentioned explicitly. But in any case the idea in question seems to have been current in later Platonism, so that it is quite understandable that Calcidius finds it necessary to combat it strongly. In order to elucidate his point of view I remind the reader of the passages from Hierocles quoted above (p. 43). Now W. Theiler has written a very

---

[2] Cf. Proclus *Comm. in Tim.* III 323, 22-23 Diehl, where among other subjects already treated by Plato in the *Republic* the author mentions τοὺς ἀγρίους ἐκείνους καὶ διαπύρους δαίμονας.

[3] R. Heinze, *Xenokrates*, p. 83 *sqq.*

interesting paper, 'Ammonios der Lehrer des Origenes',[4] in which
he tries to reconstruct the doctrine of Ammonius Saccas, teacher of
Origen and Plotinus, with the help of texts taken from Origen and
Hierocles. In both authors the world is divided into different circles
('Ringe'). About Origen Theiler says: "Unser Ausgangstext [5] stellt
den Schöpfergott der Welt gegenüber. Die Welt besteht aus dem
Ring der Gestirne mit ihren verschiedenen Rängen (zuhöchst die
Sonne), aus dem Ring der Engel mit ihren von Paulus festgelegten
Rängen, (wird hier aus christlichem Empfinden heraus vorausge-
nommen), den Ring der Menschen, auch sie gestuft nach den Rängen der Volkszugehörigkeit. Den drei Arten der *naturae rationabiles*
(φύσεις λογικαί) steht, sozusagen in einer untersten Sphäre die der
muta (ἄλογα) gegenüber".[6] These same circles can be found in
Hierocles: in the text quoted above (p. 43) the circles were allotted
to οὐράνια, αἰθέρια and περίγεια respectively.[7] Theiler is convinced
that it is possible to reconstruct Ammonius' thoughts from Hierocles: "So steht nichts im Wege, dass wir aus Hierokles das System
des Ammonios herstellen".[8] So Ammonius would be the real *auctor*
of the system of circles, which his pupil Origen used, although with
an important difference from his master: "Die Ringe bei Ammonios
sind wie durch Schotten voneinander abgesperrt, die Menschenseele
kann nicht Dämon, der Dämon nicht Gott werden und umgekehrt".[9]
For Theiler's arguments and the texts he quotes in order to prove
his views I refer to his article;[10] suffice it for our purpose to con-

---

[4] W. Theiler, *Forschungen zum Neuplatonismus* (Berlin 1966), pp. 1-45.

[5] I.e. Origen *De principiis* 168.12-169.1 Koetschau.

[6] W. Theiler, *o.c.*, p. 6.

[7] The immediate sequel to this text runs as follows: καὶ τῶν μὲν ὑποβεβη-
κότων τὰ προηγούμενα ἀεὶ ἡγεῖσθαι, πάντων δὲ βασιλεύειν τὸν ποιητὴν αὐτῶν
Θεὸν καὶ Πατέρα (Photius *Cod.* 251, 461b18-20, p. 192 Henry). This hier-
archical order recalls Calcidius' similar principle in ch. 132: *ut enim deus iuxta
angelum, sic angelus iuxta hominem* (174.4). The polemical anti-gnostic tenet,
that the highest god is also the creator, does not concern us in this connection.

[8] Theiler, *o.c.*, p. 39.

[9] Theiler, *o.c.*, p. 30.

[10] Theiler's thesis has been rather severely criticized by A. C. Lloyd
(Class. Rev. XVIII, 1968, pp. 295-297) and A. H. Armstrong (Gnomon XL,
1968, pp. 204-206); cf. especially Armstrong's verdict: "We must conclude
that this learned and brilliant attempt at reconstruction has not succeeded".
It would seem to me that neither of these critics has done full justice to
Theiler's learnedness and brilliance, which of course was outside the scope
of a book review. I should rather be inclined to subscribe to the cautious
words of A. R. Sodano: "Il lavoro di W. Theiler rappresenta, in questo

clude that Calcidius may have used a treatise in which the older
tenets of Middle-Platonism on this important point were firmly
rejected with the help of ideas which may have been developed and
taught by Ammonius. I prefer to postpone any further conclusions
to the epilogue. In the present text the cosmological hierarchy is
based on the chronological order of cosmogony as sketched in the
Timaeus; cf. Waszink's note *ad loc.* TAMEN Notwithstanding the
truth of the dogma of hierarchy, some human souls may still reach
the spheres where the demons abide. So after all (ps.) Pythagoras
was not wholly wrong. The mistake made by the Platonists criticized in the present chapter is the identification of demons and
bodiless souls. The demons are corporeal, although their bodies have
a special character: they are eternal, and so the demons have no
need to change them: (*daemon*) *non mutat corpus aliud ex alio, sed
eodem semper utitur* (175.19-20). Van der Horst in his commentary
on l. 70 of the Golden Verses quotes some interesting examples of
the belief that aether is the sphere to which the souls travel after
the breaking of earthly bounds. TRINAM This refers to the privi-
leged treatment of the philosophic soul, which regains its wings and
thus escapes the wheel of birth after 3000 years, whereas other souls
have to wait 10.000 years: 'Such a soul, if with three revolutions of
a thousand years she has thrice chosen this philosophic life, regains
thereby her wings, and speeds away after three thousand years'
(Plato, *Phaedr.* 249a3-5).

---

senso, un contributo notevolissimo, forte decisivo'' (A. R. Sodano in his
review in Riv. di Fil. e di Istruz. Classica XLV, 1967, pp. 347-352). In any
case it must be said that Theiler is not a rash revolutionary; cf. H. Langerbeck, *The Philosophy of Ammonius Saccas*, JHS 77, 1967, pp. 67-74, and
K. O. Weber, *Origenes der Neuplatoniker* (München 1962).

CONCLUSION

Calcidius' demonology, as expounded in ch. 127-136 of his *Commentarius*, quite often puts the reader in mind of the *Epinomis*, the 'thirteenth book' of Plato's *Laws*, which most scholars consider to be a spurious addition to the *corpus Platonicum*. For our purpose this vexed question is not relevant: Calcidius himself obviously thinks the *Epinomis* is a work of Plato. The importance of the dialogue for Calcidius' demonology can easily be seen even at a momentary glance at *Index* II D of Waszink's edition, which shows that the passage 981c-985c is quoted — or at least referred to — fifteen times in the *tractatus de daemonibus*. There are only two other places in the *Commentarius* in which the author clearly refers to the text of the *Epinomis*, both at the beginning of ch. 254.

That chapter treats of that class of dreams *quae diuina prouidentia uel caelestium potestatum amore iuxta homines oboriuntur* (262.19-20). The cause of such dreams, according to Calcidius, can be found in the *Epinomis*, where it is shown that the *diuinae potestates* take care of us. These *potestates* of course are the demons of the demonological paragraphs 127-136. So in fact the first part of ch. 254 is merely repeating the doctrine expounded in these paragraphs. The purpose of the pages of the *Epinomis* to which Calcidius so often refers, greatly differs from the argument of the Latin author. As is well-known, the subject of the *Epinomis* is wisdom. There is only one science which can really lead to this goal: 'that which has given the knowledge of number' (976e2). This knowledge is a gift from heaven; the orderly movements of the stars have taught man to count and to make use of number. Without number, there would be nothing but confusion and disorder. Knowledge of number helps us to reach the highest wisdom, which is piety. For this purpose a better account of the gods is needed than was given by men of old: 'since the men of old gave such a bad version of the generation of gods and creatures, my first business, I presume, must be to imagine the process better' (980c7-9). The criticism directed at 'the men of old' may in the end be the origin of the fierce attack launched by Calcidius on the way of thinking of the *prisci* in ch. 128 (see above p. 16). In contrast to that chapter, however, this criticism is not further specified. In the *Epinomis* the author's attention is first and foremost directed to the visible star-gods, who, although the all time-honoured worship of the traditional gods may—indeed, should —remain unimpaired, ought to receive the greatest honour and worship by man. These star-gods are one kind of ζῷα, in fact they are the highest class of beings; at the other end of the hierarchy are the beings of an earthly nature, and between these two categories there is a big difference: 'the earthy sort moving in disorderly fashion, that of fire with utter uniformity' (982a6-7). Orderly movement, which is always the same, is a sure sign of rationality, contrary to the usual opinion, which holds this state of affairs to be a proof of lifelessness ('we fancy them to have no souls', 982d4) and lack of reason ('deity, because it keeps to the same orbits, is unintelligent,' 982d6-7). The ideas just summarized have a certain resemblance to ch. 130, although the way of reasoning in that chapter should rather be ascribed to Aristotle, as we have seen above (p. 23). The visible star-gods are deserving of the highest honours; they take first place in the order of the world: 'after them and below them, come in order the demons and the creatures of the air' (984d8-e1). The words just quoted are the start of a very short paragraph devoted to the middle beings (984e-985c). This paragraph, which in the *Epinomis* has no special emphasis—there above all attention is paid to the visible star-gods—, obviously forms the ultimate background for Calcidius' reflections; indications for this are e.g. the middle position of the demons, the literal quotation in ch. 133, and above all the fact that the body of one class of demons mainly consists of aether, which in the *Epinomis* is the *second* of the *five* elements. This last fact, viz. that there are five elements, of which aether takes the *second* place *after* fire, is typical of the *Epinomis*. I do not know of any work in which the same hierarchy of the (five) elements and of beings belonging to the various spheres is presented as in the *Epinomis*. In Calcidius' demonological treatise the data provided in the brief paragraph just mentioned are elaborated into a more or less complete system of demonology.

Calcidius' direct source may very well have been Porphyry, as is probable for a considerable part of the *Commentarius*. Concerning the present subject we have found a significant indication for a Porphyrian authorship in ch. 135, viz. page 176.7-9 (see above p. 42). It does not seem likely, however, that Porphyry, if indeed he is the direct source, has designed the system in question himself. Our working hypothesis would rather be that a treatise by an earlier

author has been adapted by him. In my 'Calcidius on Fate' I have
tried to make plausible that such was the course of events in the
case of Calcidius' *tractatus de fato* (ch. 142-190): there a Middle-
Platonic doctrine of fate, in all probability current in the school of
Gaius, has been used and adapted in a Neo-Platonic sense.

The investigation into the possible sources for the *tractatus de fato*
was facilitated by the fact that a Middle-Platonic treatise on fate,
falsely ascribed to Plutarch, was available. The first part of Calcidius' argument shows many parallels with that treatise, which thus
provided a good starting-point for further examination. In the case
of the demonological chapters, however, such a parallel text is
lacking. There is no Middle-Platonic work which resembles Calcidius'
argument on a scale comparable with the resemblances between the
first chapters of Calcidius' *De fato* and ps. Plutarch's *De fato*. But
this does not mean that there are no indications to be found in any
Middle-Platonic writing. In fact apart from resemblances on points
of less importance, which cannot be adduced as proofs in themselves,
there are two very important elements in Calcidius' *tractatus* which
have a notable similarity to Middle-Platonic ideas.

The first of these is the passive nature of the demons, the logical
necessity of which is expounded in ch. 131. The way of reasoning
in that chapter strongly reminds us of the exposition in Maximus
Tyrius' second essay on demonology (see above p. 27). Maximus
Tyrius in this context uses the verb κοινωνεῖν, whereas Calcidius
makes use of the term *conectere*. But, exactly as in Maximus' theory,
this passive nature, which is one of the aspects of the middle position
of the demons, is not merely postulated on logical grounds in order
to arrive at a nicely balanced cosmological system, in which harmony is the binding element. The passibility has a very definite
purpose. In ch. VI of his essay Maximus contends that the soul
having stripped itself of body and having fled ἐνθένδε ἐκεῖσε, owing
to its compassion on 'kindred souls still roaming about the earth'
and thanks to its φιλανθρωπία wants to act in sympathy with the
lot of men, to help and protect them, or, if necessary, to inflict
punishment. It is worth while now to quote the first lines of ch.
VII, the final paragraph of Maximus' short λόγος: 'Not every demon
however, fulfils all tasks: each of them has a different one allotted
to itself. Now this is actually the 'affective element', by which a
demon falls short of a god. For they do not want to be wholly
released from the nature they had, when they were on the earth'.

Asclepius, Heracles, Dionysus, Amphilochus and others are cited as examples of the last statement. Of course this aspect is not relevant for Calcidius, and another important point in Maximus' demonology is even firmly rejected by him in ch. 136, viz. the theory that the demons are souls devoid of body. But the connection between passibility and concern for mankind is clearly made by Maximus in the text just quoted: τοῦτο ἐστιν ἀμέλει τὸ ἐμπαθές: τοῦτο recapitulates the different ways the demons are looking after man.

We may even take a step further. It seems rather surprising that a soul freed from body is still subject to passivity, a quality which one would rather expect to be ascribed to body, or to the combination of body and soul. It seems that Maximus somehow senses this difficulty, for he explains the passivity of the soul-demons as a kind of reminiscence of their former nature, which they do not want to renounce completely: ὡς γὰρ εἶχον φύσεως, ὅτε περὶ γῆν ἦσαν, οὐκ ἐθέλουσιν ταύτης παντάπασιν ἀπαλλάττεσθαι. Possibly we are justified in concluding that Maximus has combined two demonological dogmata, viz. 1. the demons are souls which have escaped the prison of the body, and 2. the demons have a passive nature and by reason of that they take care of man, two dogmata which originally cannot have belonged together, as the second is out of tune with the first. Now it need not cause surprise that Maximus makes such a philosophical mistake; he certainly is not a first-rate philosopher, but rather a "conférencier platonicien", as Lebreton calls him,[1] an orator who takes his subjects from philosophy, religion, ethics and the like. This fact certainly does not make Maximus' work a less reliable testimony of Middle-Platonic doctrine. On the contrary, it rather underlines the importance of that doctrine in the spiritual climate of the second century A.D.

I think it justified to conclude that the doctrine which bases the demons' providential care on their passibility (patibile propterea quia consulit, Calc. Comm. 175.20) was a Middle-Platonic dogma, and that this dogma was preserved in a 'purer' form by Calcidius than was done by Maximus.

The second passage which is worthy of closer attention is the

---

[1] J. Lebreton, Histoire du dogme de la Trinité des origines au concile de Nicée, II (Paris 1928), p. 63. The author takes this term in a rather pejorative sense, which does not do enough justice to Maximus. Lebreton is quoted in an interesting Forschungsbericht by E. des Places: Études récentes sur le platonisme moyen du IIe siècle après J.-C., Bulletin de l'Association Guillaume Budé, IVe série, 1974, pp. 347-358.

concluding definition given by Calcidius at the beginning of ch. 135. This definition, as we have seen, is very similar to the one given by Apuleius in ch. 14 of his *De deo Socratis*: *quippe, ut fine comprehendam, daemones sunt genere animalia, ingenio rationabilia, animo passiua, corpore aëria, tempore aeterna*. Apart from any difference in the details, there is a general observation to be made which in my opinion is rather important. As I have stated in the notes on ch. 135a (see above p. 38), Calcidius not unjustly presents his definition as a conclusion of his argument. Indeed his argument gives cause for some surprise, and at certain points the suspicion of faults and misunderstandings forces itself upon the reader. But that does not alter the fact that Calcidius' purpose was to present a systematic account, which he finally winds up with the definition. Put shortly, he is fully entitled to use the concluding particle *ergo* in this summary. Apuleius, on the other hand, although he pays attention to many aspects of demonology, certainly does not present a systematic account of the subject which with inevitable logic leads up to a definition. His *ut fine comprehendam* is a rhetorical rather than a logical end of his argument. Now Beaujeu in his commentary *ad loc.* makes an interesting remark about Apuleius' definition. Having quoted some parallel texts for *passiua* and *aeterna*, he says: "Quant aux autres traits énumérés par Apulée—*animalia, rationabilia, aeria* —ils résument sous une forme frappante des notions banales; cette liste est certainement tirée d'un 'catéchisme' platonicien".[2] Apuleius is no more a real philosopher than his Greek contemporary Maximus. But his philosophical works are no less important, for they provide us with summaries of Middle-Platonic philosophy. The *De deo Socratis* shows all the characteristics of the rhetorical interests and purposes of its author, but this does not take away anything from the reliability of its information about Middle-Platonic dogmata. In fact it seems quite plausible that Apuleius used a Platonic 'catéchisme', a systematic treatise, in which the definition he presents in ch. 14 indeed was a conclusion and not a mere rhetorical device.

Bearing in mind these data I do not think it rash to venture the suggestion that Maximus Tyrius, Apuleius, and the author who was Calcidius' direct source all had a systematic Middle-Platonic work on demonology at their disposal. It is unlikely that all three authors drew on exactly the same work. In any case the 'Calcidian' author

---

[2] *Apulée, opuscules philosophiques et fragments*, texte établi, traduit et commenté par J. Beaujeu (Paris 1973), p. 228.

built his treatise on the paragraph taken from the *Epinomis* to which we have paid attention above.

If it is right to postulate a Middle-Platonic treatise on demonology as the ultimate source of Calcidius' pages on this subject, it should at once be added that such a treatise cannot have been Calcidius' direct source. This is obvious from the Porphyrian phrase in ch. 135: *Exsanguium quoque simulacrorum umbraticas formas induuntur obesi corporis illuuiem trahentes* (176.7-9; see above p. 41). It is highly unlikely that such a statement belongs to Middle-Platonic thought: the 'pneuma' which is meant in the phrase just quoted is a Neo-Platonic entity.

In my opinion, the working hypothesis that a treatise by an earlier author has been adapted, has proved to be acceptable. Next we have to consider the question who has made this adaption. On account of the inquiries made by Waszink and others into various parts of the *Commentarius* and also because of the unambiguous character of the text just quoted it is only natural to assume Porphyry's authorship.

It would be out of place here to present a full review of Porphyry's philosophy, as far as it is known. For such a review I refer to Beutler's article in the *Realencyklopädie* and the collection of studies devoted to Porphyry's philosophy in the series *Entretiens sur l'Antiquité classique*.[3] Although amongst the titles of Porphyry's works there is no mention of a study which is exclusively devoted to demonology, there cannot be any doubt that Porphyry took great interest in this subject. Apart from the passages from his works which presently will be mentioned, the following remark made by Eusebius is worth recording: 'For he of all the philosophers of our time seems to have been the most familiar with demons and those whom he calls gods' (Euseb. *praep. evang.* IV 6, p. 176.14-16 Mras).

Right at the start of the *Letter to Anebo* Porphyry says: 'I shall make a start with my friendship for you by mentioning the gods and the good demons and philosophic thoughts akin to them' (p. 2.11-12 Sodano). Long before that letter, in his treatise Περὶ τῆς ἐκ λογίων φιλοσοφίας, which deals with various religious practises such as theurgy, he had spoken about gods and demons. Bidez speaks rather disapprovingly of "ce manuel de magie".[4] In the *De regressu*

---

[3] R. Beutler, *Porphyrios*, RE XXII[1], col. 275-313. *Entretiens sur l'Antiquité classique*, t. XII (Geneva 1965).

[4] J. Bidez, *Vie de Porphyre* (Leipzig 1913), p. 18.

animae, too, the demons obviously had a large part to play. In the
10th book of his *De ciuitate Dei* St. Augustine refers to some of the
doctrines present in this study. Concerning the demons Porphyry
is said to have discerned *a daemonibus angelos, aeria loca esse daemonum, aetheria uel empyria disserens angelorum* (ch. 9). Unfortunately
it is not clear how the abode of the angels, if indeed this is Porphyry's
and not Augustine's term, is related to the star-gods, who, one
would think, must be located in the sphere of fire. The angels,
however, are also said to belong to that domain: the expression
aetheria uel empyria [5] points to an equation of aether and fire. Such
an equation also seems to be present in a remark in the *Letter to
Anebo*, to which Iamblichus is replying in his *De mysteriis*. Porphyry
apparently proposed that the differences between gods, demons and
human souls are due to the difference of their bodily structure.
Iamblichus protests: οὐ μέντοι τὴν ὑπὸ σοῦ διάκρισιν ὑποτεινομένην αὐτῶν προσιέμεθα, ἥτις τὴν πρὸς τὰ διαφέροντα σώματα κατάταξιν, οἷον
θεῶν μὲν πρὸς τὰ αἰθέρια, δαιμόνων δὲ πρὸς τὰ ἀέρια, ψυχῶν δὲ τῶν περὶ
γῆν, αἰτίαν εἶναί φησι τῆς νυνὶ ζητουμένης διαστάσεως (*De mysteriis*
I 8, p. 51, 9-13 des Places).[6] In this case the gods are said to reside
in the ethereal or fiery sphere, which is normal doctrine. It cannot
be deduced from the references to *De regressu animae* what the exact
composition of the hierarchy of beings was in that book. It would
seem, however, that it differed considerably from the doctrine
hinted at in the *Letter to Anebo*. In the last-mentioned work Porphyry must indeed have paid great attention to the hierarchy of
beings, for in the first paragraphs he is raising many questions
about the distinctions to be made within that hierarchy.

A distinction which is not explicitly present in the Greek fragments or references [7] is referred to in ch. 11 of St. Augustine's *De
ciuitate Dei* X, where the following is said about Porphyry's demonology in the *Letter to Anebo*: *quosdam namque benignos daemones more*

---

[5] Like its Greek original the transcribed adjective *empyrius* according to
the *Thesaurus* is found in only very few Latin texts, one of which is worth
quoting here, viz. Marius Victorinus *In ep. ad Gal.* 4, 9. In that paragraph
the author is commenting on the expressions *egena elementa huius mundi*:
. . . . *deinde etiam quosdam daemones aerios uocent, rursus alii empyrios, alii
enydros, alii geinos, id est terrenos, aquaticos, ignitos, aerios* (p. 47.13-15
Locher). So in this text there is even mentioned a fiery class of demons.
[6] In his edition of the *Letter* A. R. Sodano proposes the following conjecture: ψυχῶν δὲ τῶν περὶ <κοσμίων πρὸς τὰ περὶ> γῆν (p. 3.14-15).
[7] The following words concern the heavenly gods: ἡ δ' ἐξῆς ἐπιζήτησις ἡ
σὴ διαπορεῖ, πῶς αὐτῶν οἱ μέν εἰσιν ἀγαθοποιοί, οἱ δὲ κακοποιοί (p. 7.1-2 Sodano).

appellat aliorum, cum omnes generaliter inprudentes esse fateatur. Apparently Porphyry in the *Letter* distinguished bad demons from good ones. Proclus also reports that Porphyry made such a distinction: one class was formed by the ὑλικαὶ δυνάμεις or the ὑλικοὶ δαίμονες (Proclus, *comm. in Tim.* I 77.19-20 and 171.21 Diehl). One is tempted to connect ὑλικός with the Calcidian phrase *habent nimiam cum silua communionem* (176.11). However that may be, the distinction between wicked and benevolent demons is very prominent in the only systematic account of Porphyry's demonology available to us, viz. *De abstinentia* II 37-43. In fact the distinction between δαίμονες ἀγαθοί and δαίμονες κακοεργοί is the real subject of Porphyry's account in these chapters. The demons are said to live in the sublunary spheres: so their nature, one may suppose, is not fiery. Now the one and only reason for the difference between the two classes of demons, the good and the bad, is their mastery or lack of mastery of their πνεῦμα. Those which are in control of that entity are good, those which τοῦ συνεχοῦς πνεύματος οὐ κρατοῦσιν, ἀλλ' ὡς τὸ πολὺ καὶ κρατοῦνται are wicked (see above p. 41). All this can be found in ch. 38. By way of introduction in ch. 37 Porphyry provides a short sketch of the higher stages in the divine hierarchy, viz. the first, unbodily God, the World-Soul, and the visible gods. The other chapters (39-43) enlarge upon the distinction between good and bad demons, mainly in a practical, warning sense. There are no real additions to the theory; everything is meant to warn the reader against the influences of the wicked demons, who are constantly trying to pull man from the right path both in his thoughts and especially in his religious practises. The following quotation aptly summarizes the character of the demonological digression; speaking about the wicked demons Porphyry says: 'Deceit is their speciality: for they want to be gods and the power at the head of them wants to be considered the highest god. These are the beings rejoicing at 'drink-offering and the odour of fat', by which their pneumatic and bodily parts are fattened. For these parts live on the vapours and exhalations in a manifold way and are strengthened by the odours from blood and meat. Therefore a wise and prudent man will beware of such beings and he will be eager to purify his soul in all manners, for they do not attack a pure soul because of the dissimilarity with themselves' (Porphyry, *De abstinentia* II 42-43, p. 171.22-172.11 Nauck). I think these words clearly indicate Porphyry's purpose in this digression. He is often interested in the practical implications of a theory; and the demonological paragraphs are of course closely bound up with the real subject of the treatise: abstinence from meat. This subject was directly related to the Ancients' practises of sacrifice etc., and for that reason the demonological digression was inserted. Now this is precisely the problem we are confronted with in studying Porphyry's demonological tenets. In so far as indications of these tenets can be found, these are always put forward within the framework of studies of another kind, such as theurgy, magic, religion, etc. This greatly reduces our possibilities of reconstructing Porphyry's doctrine. An even greater restriction, however, lies in the simple fact that the texts available belong to different phases of Porphyry's long career as a philosopher. Add to this the uncertainties as to the precise stages of this career and it is clear that a reconstruction of Porphyrian demonology is a precarious undertaking. One thing is certain, viz., that Porphyry took a great interest in this domain of religion and philosophy, mainly, as we have seen, for practical purposes, which does not mean that theoretical systematization left him cold. In the fragments of the *Letter to Anebo* e.g. we read: 'This, too, has to be made clear to you, in which respect a demon differs from a *heros* and a soul concerning its essence, potentiality or actuality. For you are seeking after the token of the presence of a god, an angel, an archangel, a demon, a power or a soul' (*Ep. ad Anebo* p. 7.8-11 Sodano). Such a quotation, it would seem to me, is characteristic of Porphyry's interests, which are both practical and theoretical.

As to the problem we are trying to solve, viz. to find the source(s) of Calcidius' *tractatus de daemonibus*, the first conclusion to be drawn would be that it is quite possible that Porphyry was interested in a systematic treatise about demons. Put in another way: there is no *a priori* improbability in considering Porphyry to be Calcidius' direct source. This naturally is only a very general consideration which in itself lacks any demonstrative force. Slightly more important is the fact that Porphyry without doubt paid much attention to the class of evil demons. This may not be typical solely of his philosophy, but on the other hand e.g. his teacher Plotinus lacks such a preoccupation. It is true that Calcidius does not pay much attention to the wicked spirits; above all his thoughts are bent towards the salutary activities of the good demons. This is quite understandable in view of his addressee. But the evil demons certainly are not absent from the treatise: the second part of ch. 135 is devoted to them. The extremely condensed state of the information which is provided in that paragraph may very well be the abstract of a much more extensive treatment in Calcidius' source. The contents of ch. 135b can by no means be considered to be incompatible with Porphyry's ideas in this matter; on the contrary there are some obvious similarities, some of which are highly significant: indeed apart from any other details the most important indication of Porphyrian provenance is the phrase in ch. 135 discussed above (see above p. 40). This phrase seems to me the decisive proof of Porphyry's authorship.

I should like to add the following to this conclusion. One of the most characteristic elements in Calcidius' *tractatus* is the presence of *aether* as a fifth element on the *second* step of the ladder formed by the cosmic hierarchy. This of course is due to the starting-point provided by the passage of the *Epinomis* mentioned above. As far as I know, in Porphyry's other works there is no indication of such a state of affairs. It is worth while to return once more to Hierocles. In the system sketched in his works the highest place in the cosmic order is taken by the Demiurge. Behind him are the three λογικαὶ φύσεις: put in the wording of his comments on the Pythagorean *Golden Verses*: ἀθάνατοι θεοί, ἀγαυοὶ ἥρωες, ἀνθρώπιναι ψυχαί. Now the ἀθάνατοι θεοί are the οὐράνια in Photius' summary (see above p. 43), whereas the ἀγαυοὶ ἥρωες (which is the name in the *Golden Verses* Hierocles is commenting upon) without any doubt are the equivalents of the αἰθέριοι or δαίμονες ἥρωες in the summary. About these ἥρωες ἀγαυοί Hierocles provides some very interesting further information, which it is worth to quote literally: Οἱ δὴ καὶ εἰκότως ἀγαυοὶ ἥρωες λέγονται, ἀγαυοὶ μὲν ὡς ἀγαθοὶ ὄντες καὶ φωτεινοὶ ἀεὶ καὶ μὴ ἐν κακίᾳ μήτε ἐν λήθῃ ποτὲ γινόμενοι, ἥρωες δὲ ὡς ἔρωές τινες ὄντες καὶ ἥρωες οἷον ἐρωτικοὶ καὶ διαλεκτικοὶ ἐρασταὶ τοῦ θεοῦ αἴροντες ἡμᾶς καὶ κουφίζοντες πρὸς τὴν θείαν πολιτείαν ἀπὸ τῆς ἐν γῇ διατριβῆς. Τοὺς δὲ αὐτοὺς καὶ δαίμονας ἀγαθοὺς καλεῖν ἔθος, ὡς ὄντας δαήμονας καὶ ἐπιστήμονας τῶν θείων νόμων, ἔστι δὲ ὅτε καὶ ἀγγέλους ὡς ἐκφαίνοντας καὶ διαστέλλοντας ἡμῖν τοὺς πρὸς εὐζωίαν κανόνας (Hierocles, *comm. in aur. Pyth. carmen* p. 19.9-17 Koehler); in paraphrase: "These are suitably called 'noble heroes', 'noble', because they are good and always brightly clear, never involved in wickedness nor in forgetfulness, 'heroes', because, being a kind of 'loves', as amorous and philosophical lovers of God they are exalting and raising us from our earthly dwellings towards the divine republic. It is also customary to call these same beings 'demons', as they are skilled in the divine laws, sometimes also 'messengers', because they reveal and command the rules for well-being". In this passage Hierocles, among other things by the use of the weapon of etymology, so beloved by philosophers both in Antiquity and in modern times, is explaining how the ἥρωες ἀγαυοί of the *Golden Verses* are indeed the middle beings of traditional Platonic thought. The immediate sequel to the text just quoted is extremely interesting: πολλάκις δὲ καὶ ταῖς τρισὶν ἐπινοίαις χρώμενοι τὸ πλάτος τοῦ μέσου γένους εἰς τρία τέμνομεν καὶ τὸ μὲν προσεχὲς τοῖς οὐρανίοις καλοῦμεν ἀγγέλους, τὸ δὲ τοῖς ἐπιγείοις συναπτόμενον ἥρωας καὶ τὸ ἐξ ἴσου τῶν ἄκρων ἀμφοτέρων ἀπέχον δαίμονας, ὥσπερ πολλαχοῦ ποιεῖ Πλάτων (*id.* p. 19.17-22): "But often, making use of the three conceptions (just mentioned), we also divide the (whole) range of the middle class into three parts, and we call the class next to the heavenly sphere 'messengers' ('angels'), the group bordering on the terrestrial 'heroes' and the class at equal distance from both extremities 'demons', as Plato does in many places". So it is permitted to put forward the following hierarchy:

1. ἀθάνατοι θεοί
---
2. ἄγγελοι
3. δαίμονες
4. ἥρωες
---
5. ἀνθρώπιναι ψυχαί

There is an unmistakable likeness between this scheme and the order of five classes, three of them belonging together more closely, which we have found in Calcidius, the more so, when we bear in mind the appellation αἰθέρια used for the (whole? of the) middle group.[8] So the highest class is raised above the sphere of aether, and thus it would seem unlikely that Hierocles equated fire and aether. His highest class, the ἀθάνατοι θεοί, must be the well-known star-gods, and the supposition seems justified that he considered these to be of a fiery nature. About the nature of Hierocles' aether not much can be learned. In his comments on the last two of the *Golden Verses* he calls it a ἄυλον καὶ ἀίδιον σῶμα (p. 120.7 Koehler), but one should be rather careful in drawing conclusions. Hierocles

---

[8] But possibly only the ἄγγελοι belong to αἰθήρ, *cf.* τὸ μὲν προσεχὲς τοῖς οὐρανίοις καλοῦμεν ἀγγέλους (p. 19.19-20 Koehler) and τόπος ὁ ὑπὸ σελήνην προσεχῶς .... ὃν αἰθέρα ἐλεύθερον οἱ Πυθαγόρειοι καλοῦσιν (p. 120.4-7).

is commenting on the Pythagorean text and it does not necessarily follow that he himself would have used the term for the domain in question. A striking parallel may be found in the comments on the third of the *Golden Verses* (τούς τε καταχθονίους σέβε δαίμονας, ἔννομα ῥέζων), where the καταχθόνιοι δαίμονες are shown to be the third class in the hierarchy, viz. ἄνθρωποι! With this reservation in mind we may still gladly accept some further information about Hierocles' aether. In a sentence immediately preceding the definition just quoted he speaks about the place to which the soul travels after its purification: .... τόπος ὁ ὑπὸ σελήνην προσεχῶς, ὡς ὑπερέχων μὲν τῶν φθαρτῶν σωμάτων, ὑποβεβηκὼς δὲ τῶν οὐρανίων, ὃν αἰθέρα ἐλεύθερον οἱ Πυθαγόρειοι καλοῦσιν (p. 120.4-7 Koehler): "a place directly beneath the moon, as it is above the corruptible bodies, but beneath the heavenly, a place which the Pythagoreans call 'free aether' ". For the moment I confine myself to the observation that Hierocles taught a hierarchy of five classes of rational beings, which five classes can also be classified into a *tri*partition, because the three middle classes belong closely together. For the middle classes αἰθήρ is mentioned as their specific nature, and αἰθήρ is one of the sublunary parts of the kosmos.[9]

Let us now turn to Hierocles' further comments on the contents of the *Golden Verses* 70 and 71. In my notes on ch. 136 (see above p. 50) I referred to a paper by W. Theiler, in which Hierocles was quoted as a testimony of the doctrine of Ammonius Saccas. An extremely important tenet of this doctrine is the sharp separation between the spheres in the world order. It may be useful to repeat a quotation from Theiler's article: ".... die Menschenseele kann nicht Dämon, der Dämon nicht Gott werden und umgekehrt".[10] It is fascinating to observe, how Hierocles has tried to combine his great awe for the text of the *Golden Verses* with the tenet just quoted from Theiler's description, a tenet which seems to be in flat contra-

---

[9] Cf. Proclus *comm. in Crat.* p. 75.9-76.19 Pasquali, where it is both stated that the three middle classes may be taken together under the collective noun δαίμονες (p. 76.16) and each class is given its own name with an etymological explanation, ἄγγελος of course speaking for itself, ἥρως, as in Hierocles, related to the verb αἴρειν, whereas for δαίμων yet another etymological derivation is presented, viz. from δαίζειν ('to divide', synonymous with μερίζειν); cf. also Proclus *comm. in Tim. III* p. 165.11 *sqq.* Diehl. Other etymological associations are δαήμων (Plato) and δειμαίνειν (Eusebius). Modern dictionaries connect δαίμων with δαίεσθαι in the sense 'to allot', 'to assign'.

[10] W. Theiler, *o.c.*, p. 40.

diction with this text. Man, he says, can certainly reach the high goal mentioned in the Pythagorean text, which goal is φιλοσοφίας ὁ τελειότατος καρπός (p. 119.6-7 Koehler). But one should not misunderstand this perfection: οὐ γὰρ δὴ τὸ τρίτον γένος τελειωθὲν ἢ τοῦ μέσου γένοιτ' ἄν κρεῖττον ἢ τῷ πρώτῳ ἴσον, ἀλλὰ μένον τρίτον ὁμοιοῦται τῷ πρώτῳ γένει ὑποτεταγμένον τῷ μέσῳ (p. 120.22-25 Koehler): "For the third class will never, although rendered perfect, become superior to the middle or equal to the first, but staying third it becomes like the first, being subordinated to the middle". This is in full accordance with this general adage: ἀκροτάτη δὲ ἀρετὴ τοῖς τε τῆς δημιουργίας ὅροις ἐμμένειν, οἷς πάντα κατ' εἶδος διακέκριται, καὶ τοῖς τῆς προνοίας ἔπεσθαι νόμοις, δι' οὓς τὰ πάντα κατὰ τὴν οἰκείαν δύναμιν πρὸς τὸ σύμμετρον ἀγαθὸν οἰκειοῦται (p. 121.14-18 Koehler): "The consummate virtue is to remain within the bounds of creation, by which (bounds) all things are distinguished according to their kind, and to obey the laws of Providence, by which (laws) all things, in accordance with their proper capacity, are made to be like the good commensurate to them". Such thoughts cannot be found in Calcidius' concluding chapter 136, in which Hierocles' almost religious awe for the *Golden Verses* is also lacking. But Calcidius shows a fundamental agreement with Hierocles in the dogma that each class of beings remains within its own cosmic bounds. For this must be the implicit background of Calcidius' polemic directed against traditional views, and his arguments on p. 177.5-10 surely are not inspired by philological precision, but by cosmological doctrine. His final statement of ch. 136 (p. 177.10-12) seems to be the shortened version of an explanation which tries to save the text of the *Golden Verses* by a correct exegesis.

All this receives added interest, if Theiler is right indeed in assuming Ammonius Saccas to be the main source of Hierocles' thoughts and especially, if a further idea of his might also be correct, viz. a special interest taken by Porphyry in Ammonius' doctrine: "Porphyrius näherte sich in dem Masse dem Ammonios, wie sich Plotin von ihm entfernte". For this maxim Theiler adduces some impressive arguments, one of which is worth mentioning here, as it also concerns Calcidius. Hierocles explicitly rejected a migration of human souls into animals. The shortest version of his view is the following phrase about Plato: τὸν μὲν ἐξ ἀλόγων ζῴων ἢ εἰς ἄλογα μεταγγισμὸν οὐκ ἀναδεχόμενος (Hierocles *apud* Phot. cod. 214, 172b22-23, p. 128 Henry). Such a migration is also rejected by Calcidius in ch. 198 of the *Commentarius* and indeed by Porphyry, as is reported by St. Augustine in ch. 30 of the tenth book of *De ciuitate Dei*, whereas Plotinus is said to have adhered to this doctrine. It would seem that rejection originates from the providential separation of the various classes in the world order brought about by the Demiurge, the idea underlying Calcidius' remarks in ch. 136.

All this leads to the tentative conclusion that similarities between Calcidius' *tractatus de daemonibus* and tenets found in Hierocles' writings strengthen the hypothesis that Porphyry was Calcidius' source. This hypothesis presupposes that Hierocles is in fact referring to Ammonius' doctrine and that Porphyry had a predilection for that doctrine.

The following short survey is only meant to sketch a possible course of things. The Middle-Platonic treatise postulated above, or at least a doctrine similar to such a treatise, was used and elaborated by Ammonius Saccas. Porphyry took note of (some of) Ammonius' ideas and also of the treatise in question itself. He adapted this treatise adding some *Ammoniana*, especially in the polemic doxographical epilogue, and also his own doctrine of the evil demons and their πνεῦμα.[11] I fully admit the speculative character of this sketch, but perhaps not all speculation is wholly unfounded or useless...
Finally Calcidius. He faced a delicate task. Osius, his addressee, might be expected to reject any pagan demonology: in his eyes demons were evil beings. But there was a possibility of performing the task: Osius knew all about angels and about the two kinds of these beings, the bad and the good. If he could be shown that Greek philosophy in fact taught the same doctrine, pagan demonology might be acceptable after all. Thus Calcidius carefully revised his source, adding a Biblical reminiscence and working up carefully to the equation of demons and angels. This equation was not original; Philo, too, had equated demons and angels. As we have seen in the texts quoted from Porphyry and Hierocles, pagan philosophy had also used the word ἄγγελοι for (the) middle beings. This may have facilitated Calcidius' task.

---

[11] Possibly the following juxtaposition of hierarchies is of some use:

	Epinomis	Hierocles	Porphyry *apud Calc.*
fire	θεοὶ ὁρατοί	ἀθάνατοι θεοί	stellae
aether	δαίμονες	ἄγγελοι	daemones (angeli)
air	ἀέριον γένος	δαίμονες	daemones
water	ἡμίθεος	ἥρωες	daemones nocentes!
earth	ἄνθρωποι	ἄνθρωποι	homines

Could it be that Porphyry's special contribution was to put the wicked demons on the fourth place, that of the humid element?

INDEX

SOME TERMS AND SUBJECTS

aether 3, 5, 18sqq., 26, 36sqq., 39sqq., 48sqq., 50, 51, 53, 58, 61sqq.

Ammonius 6, 50, 64, 65

angels *passim*

anima maligna 44sqq.

caelum 35sqq.

daëmon 2, 30

epopticus 12

Golden Verses 6, 48sqq., 51, 61sqq.

Hebraei 24sqq., 29, 33

hierarchy in the cosmos 6, 49sqq., 53, 58, 59, 61sqq.

Middle-Platonic thought 4sqq., 14, 19, 49, 54, 55, 56, 57, 65

migration of souls 64

passivus 38, 56

patibilis 16, 26, 28, 39, 55

pneuma 6, 21, 40sqq., 57, 59

prisci 16, 17, 52

rationabilis 22, 25, 26, 38, 50, 56

silva 43

stars, star-gods 19, 20, 21, 22sqq., 53, 58, 62

ultor 42, 43, 49

wicked demons 4, 6, 32sqq., 39sqq., 59, 60

MODERN SCHOLARS

Andres, F. 29n

Arnaldez, R. 24

Armstrong, A. H. 50n

Beaujeu, J. 42n, 56

Beutler, R. 42n, 57

Bidez, J. 57

Boeft, J. den 43n, 54

Courcelle, P. 31n

Cumont, F. 29n

Dillon, J. M. 13n

Dodds, E. R. 42n

Dörrie, H. 3

Frisk, H. 37

Heinze, R. 3, 42n, 49

Jaeger, W. 23

Kirchmeyer, J. 12n

Klibansky, R. 13n

Langerbeck, H. 51n

Lebreton, J. 55n

Leemans, E.-A. 43n, 45

Lloyd, A. C. 50n

Lobeck, C. A. 12

Mangenot, E. 33n

Michl, J. 29n, 33n

Nat, P. G. van der 32n, 33n

Novotny, F. 15

Pease, A. S. 17n

Places, E. des 43n, 45, 55n

Portogalli, B. M. 42n

Regen, F. 42n

Rose, H. J. 23n

Sodano, A. R. 50n

Soury, G. 4n

Taylor, A. E. 11n, 14

Theiler, W. 49, 50, 63, 64

Waszink, J. H. *passim*

Weber, K. O. 51n

Winden, J. C. M. van 9n, 12n, 44

PASSAGES QUOTED OR REFERRED TO

Aetius, Placita (ed. Diels, Dox. Gr.)
    305b   40

Albinus, Epitome
    15

    5, 19, 30

Apuleius
 Apol. 43   II
 De deo Socr. 8   19
      II 37^n
      13   38
      14   56
      15   31, 47, 49

[Aristoteles]
 De mundo 392a5-9 18^n

Augustinus
 De civ. dei
    VIII 14   31
    X 9   58
    X 11   58
    X 19   33
    X 30   65
 Serm. de vet. test. (ed. Lambot)
    72.52-56   29

Calcidius (ed. Waszink)
 Transl.
    22.9   II
    34.11-12   II
    34.13-14   10
    34.13.-35.2   13
    35.11-12   37
    47.3 20^n
 Comm. (only passages not belong-
 ing to the *tractatus de daemonibus*)
    60.1   47
    72.13   21
    99.26   47
    102.10-11   38
    151.3   36
    155.12 31^n
    155.14 31^n
    165.24-25 35^n
    199.1   2
    210.20-21 31^n
    213.4   7, 43
    246.16   31
    262.19-20   52
    273.14 17^n
    277.5   12
    297.8   47
    299.14-16   44
    330.20 31^n

Cicero
 De nat. deor.
    I 38   16, 17, 17^n
    I 118   16, 17^n

[Cicero]
    II 42   23, 23^n
    II 44 23^n
    II 61 17^n
    III 63   17
 De orat. I 53   46
 Tim. (ed. Ax) 177^b II

Clemens, Strom. (ed. Stählin)
    411.7-8 29^n

Diogenes Laertius
    prol.   14
    III 74   13
    VIII 32   47

Empedocles (ed. Diels)
    fr. B 112   2, 48
    fr. B 115   2, 48

Eusebius, Praep. evang. (ed. Mras)
    175.18-21   30
    176.14-16   6, 57
    344-360   24

Heraclitus (ed. Diels)
    fr. B 119   2

Hesiodus, Opera
    122-123   I
    252-253   2

Hierocles
 comm. in aur. Pyth. carm. (ed.
 Koehler)
    19.9-17   61
    19.17-22   62
    19.19-20 62^n
    119.6-7   64
    120.4-7 62^n, 63
    120.7   62
    120.22-25   64
    121.14-18   64
 apud Photium (ed. Henry)
    cod. 214
      128   64
    cod. 251
      191   43
      192   50^n
      195   43

Homerus
 Ilias XI 792   I
 Odyss. 24, 149   I

Iamblichus, De mysteriis (ed. des Places)
51.9-13   58

Marius Victorinus, In ep. ad Gal. (ed. Locher)
47.13-15   58[n]

Maximus Tyrius (ed. Hobein)
VIII 7   4
     8   38
IX 1   27
     4   27
     6   27, 47, 54
     7   54, 55

Numenius (ed. des Places)
fr. 37   45[n]
fr. 52   43[n]

Origenes
Comm. in cant. cant. (ed. Baehrens)
     75.21-23   12[n]
Contra Cels.
     I 16   14
     V 4   31[n]
     VIII 25   33[n]
De princ. (ed. Koetschau)
     168.12-169.1   50[n]

Philo
De gigant. 6   31
De opif. mundi 58   24

Plato
Apol. 27c-d   2
Cratyl.
     397c4-398c5   2
     403a-b   37
     410b7   18[n]
Gorg. 493b5   37
Leg. 713c-d   2
Phaedo 80dsqq.   37
Phaedr. 249a3-5   51
Resp.
     615e4   49
     620d8-e1   3
     620d sqq.   49
Symp.
     202d-e   3
     202e3-6   30
     210a   12
Tim.
     32b2-3   27

[Plato]
     32d1-2   13
     40d4   10, 11
     40d6sqq.   5, 11, 14
     40d6-7   10
     41bsqq.   37
     42e8   31
     47c3   20
     49c4   20[n]
     58d1-2   20
Epin.
     976e2   52
     980c7-9   52
     981c-985c   52
     981d4-5   36
     981d7-e1   36
     982a6-7   53
     982c5-d2   24
     982d4   53
     982d6-7   53
     984c5   23
     984d8-e1   53
     984e-985c   53
     984e4-5   36
     984e5-985a2   30
     985a   27
     985b1-3   3
     985b4-7   39
Theag. 128d2-7   2

Plinius, Nat. Hist.
II 14sqq.   17[n]

Plotinus, Enn.
III 5.6   6

Plutarchus
De def. or.
     416d   4
     417b   43
     417c   4
     419c   4
     431e   47
De fac. 944c   47
De gen. Socr. 593d   4, 47
De Is. 378a   17[n]
Quaest. Rom. 276f   43

Porphyrius
De abst. (ed. Nauck)
     167.26-168.3   41
     168.4-5   6
     168.6   33
     168.7-12   40

[Porphyrius]
   171.16   34
   171.22-172.11   59
  De antro (ed. Nauck)
   64.15-18   41
   64.19-20   41
  Ep. ad An. (ed. Sodano)
   2.11-12   57
   3.14-15   58[n]
   7.1-2   58[n]
   7.8-11   60
  Sent. (ed. Lamberz)
   19.6-7   41
   19.14-20.1   41
  Vita Plot. 17   45[n]

Proclus
  Comm. in Crat. (ed. Pasquali)
   75.9-76.19   63[n]
  Comm. in Parm. (ed. Cousin)
   617.23-618.2   12[n]
  Comm. in Tim. (ed. Diehl)
   I 13.4-6   12[n]
   I 13.14-17   13[n]
   I 76.21-77.23   45[n]
   I 77.19-20   59
   I 171.21   59
   III 165.11sqq.   63[n]
   III 323.22-23   49[n]

Scriptura sacra
  Gen.
   1.14-16   24
   6.4   45
  Matth.
   18.10   30
   25.41   33
  Marc. 8.38   33[n]
  Luc. 1.19   30
  II Cor. 12.7   33
  II Petr. 2.4   45
  Jud. 6   45
  Apoc.
   12.7   33
   14.10   33[n]
Sextus Empiricus, Adv. math.
  IX 86-87   23[n]
SVF (ed. v. Arnim)
  I 448   16
  II 527, 580, 642, 664,
   1067   20[n]
  II 1008   12
  II 1076   38
Theodoretus, Graec. aff. cur.
  III 5   17
  III 49sqq.   17
Xenocrates (ed. Heinze)
  fr.15   37

Printed in the United States
By Bookmasters